BOOKS BY PHILIP DEANE

I SHOULD HAVE DIED

I
SHOULD HAVE
DIED

BY

PHILIP DEANE

(Philippe Deane Gigantes)

ATHENEUM *NEW YORK*

*1*977

Library of Congress Cataloging in Publication Data

Deane, Philip.
  I should have died.

  1. Korean War, 1950-1953—Prisoners and prisons.
  2. Korean War, 1950-1953—Personal narratives, American.
  3. Constantine II, King of the Hellenes, 1940-
  4. Deane, Philip. I. Title.
  DS921.D42 1977   951.9'042'0924   76-25896
  ISBN 0-689-10766-8

A SYLVIE MON AMOUR

Mes remerciements à Mlle
Marie-Rose Goulet qui
m'a si gentiment aidé

INTRODUCTION

In the nineteen fifties, I was a prisoner of the communists in Korea. They tried to brainwash me and to convert me. I resisted because I believed they were in the wrong; that the Americans were in the right; that in the western world, under American leadership, the individual had a chance of seeing his rights respected; and that small nations had a better chance to be free. I gave three years of my life to that belief.

In the nineteen sixties, the Americans supported a corrupt Greek dictatorship which abolished all democratic freedoms and ruled through torture and terror. I was an official of the last, legal Greek government before the dictatorship.

Like most people, I have had a life that had seemed extraordinarily out of my control, a life which plunged me to depths where I did not quite think I deserved to be and raised me to heights where I felt unsafe and did not really want to be. This was mainly due to my father Lakis Gigantes and his brother Yanis who were, in my youth, living military legends from Greece's battles in World War One and who became even more legendary in Greece during World War Two, my father as Commander of the Greek Sacred Regiment, an élite commando unit which liberated the Greek Aegean islands; my uncle as the Greek Resistance leader who stayed to burn his documents when he knew he would be caught, and died, gun in hand, after killing six of his would-be captors, one with each bullet in his .38 service revolver.

Greece has had a traumatic history this century, studded with wars, disasters, misgovernment and brutality. For many Greeks this has only increased the value of the legends that were my father and my uncle. Mr Panayotis Canellopoulos, a former Greek prime-minister, writing in the Athens newspaper *TO VIMA* in April 1975 said they were Homeric. *TO VIMA* compared my father to Bayard, the French knight 'without fear and without reproach' who lived at the end of the fifteenth and the beginning of the sixteenth century.

Now, after the shame of dictatorship, the revelations of corruption and moral weakness, many Greeks find it comforting to remember Lakis and Yanis Gigantes who remained untainted in the troubled times of recently history : all the more comforting since my father at least, was recently alive—he died in 1970, in London where he had gone because, as he said, he did not want to be buried in Greece until the land was free. This was a personal act, unnoticed anywhere in the world but Greece. Greek newspapers defied censorship to print the news. For the Greeks, who were under the yoke of the junta, my father's last personal act had the force of symbol.

To me these two men, my father and my uncle, had always been such symbols. I loved them and admired them as only a small boy can. But symbols are hard to live with and so I spent a good deal of my life fleeing them because I was expected to live up to them and I did not think I could.

It was because my father was admired by important Britons that I was given the opportunity, in World War Two, to enter the Royal Naval College. Because I was my father's son, the King of Greece himself, King George the Second, called me to Claridge's where he lived in exile and told me it would be unthinkable and an almost treasonable injury to Greece if Gigantes' son did not get top marks at the Royal Naval College.

And so ensued with my tutor, instructor Lt Wright, a conversation that went something like this :

'You are studying too hard.'

'I can't manage to keep up otherwise, sir.'

'But you do it too obviously, my dear fellow. It won't do. People are calling you a swot. This will count against you. The British will not accept open application to intellectual pursuits. It is not elegant. The effort must not show. Remember how Aeschines chided Demosthenes for declaiming speeches which smelled of midnight oil? Open application to fishing is another matter. That is admired . . .'

I took Lt Wright at his word, literally. In any kind of weather, I would go out in a dinghy, on the river, and study while pretending to fish. The fact that I rarely if ever caught anything endeared me all the more to my colleagues.

Immediately after the war I left the Navy and had a glorious period of irresponsibility in London, not worrying about success or competing.

The London *Observer* hired me as its Greek stringer at 25 pounds a month and then allowed me to go to the Korean War as their correspondent when I arranged the financing of my trip with three Greek publications.

I took foolish risks, was wounded several times and was taken prisoner by the Communists. They tried brainwashing me and gave up just when I was sure I was going to break. Thus I came out with a reputation of being unbreakable, as the son of Lakis Gigantes was bound to have been.

For David Astor, editor of the London *Observer*, I had become both a marketable byline and a guilt complex. He felt not a little guilty that I had spent thirty-three months in prison camp because I had been his correspondent at the front. So he gave me choice assignments, syndicating my articles round the world.

In 1956, the *Observer* made a deal with the *Toronto Globe and Mail* and I ended up in Washington as correspondent for both papers. In 1961, I tired of journalism and joined the United Nations, as Director of their Washington information centre. Soon, U Thant, an old acquaintance from my journalistic days, became Secretary General. And that was the job I occupied when I was summoned from Greece to become Secretary-General to young King Constantine. Why me? I do not really know. Maybe U Thant spoke highly of me to Queen Frederika. Maybe the Queen was still impressed by my alleged unbreakability under Communist brainwashing. Maybe she wanted her son to have a courtier with a well known liberal name : I believe I have said that my father was a liberal.

Then I decided to leave the King because I discovered the palace plot to overthrow the Liberal Prime Minister through an army coup. And, at that time, the Prime Minister needed someone who knew Washington's political world. So I found myself named Minister of Culture and sent to Washington as envoy extraordinary and minister plenipotentiary, to present the Greek case on Cyprus and to try convincing the Americans that they should not support the palace plot against the legally elected, majority government of the Greek people.

*

A postscript about my name : it really is GERASSIMOS GIGANTES. The London *Observer* chose for me the pen-name

PHILIP DEANE. I wrote asking why they had picked that particular byline; I had left for the Korean war before they could answer. When I came out of prison, the *Observer* people could not remember why they had given me that name . . . 'we thought of calling you Alexander Something but it sounded too Scottish,' they said. By then, my imprisonment by the Communists had given the pen-name PHILIP DEANE exposure and commercial value. So PHILIP DEANE I remained. Then, just before he died, my father asked that I return to the name GIGANTES. And I live among French Canadians who spell my name PHILIPPE. Since all those with whom I have ever worked still call me PHILIP DEANE, a good way of satisfying everyone seemed to be to take, officially, the name PHILIPPE DEANE GIGANTES. I hardly dare hope that this arrangement will put an end to the sort of situation which arose when my daughter asked me before my hotel's reception clerk : 'Daddy, which name did you register under this time?'

NOTES : Superscribed numerals refer to notes at the back of the book, on page 180.

CONTENTS

PART ONE

KOREA

It was July 23, 1950, my thirteenth day in Korea, as a war correspondent. The troops of Communist North Korea had already poured halfway down South Korea. Shells from North Korean howitzers were crashing into the town of Yongdong, disintegrating building after building. The advance headquarters of the United States First Cavalry Division was pulling out. Seven miles to the northwest, on the main road to Taejon, the 71st Tank Company under Lieutenant Bob Freeman, was covering the retreat, and this was the only force available to stem the tide of fifteen Red divisions rolling south.

Communist armour was reported moving to attack Lieutenant Freeman's force. I left headquarters by jeep to cover the engagement. Three miles out of town we came under sniper fire. We drove on. A few moments later our sump was pierced, and the engine seized. A bullet hit my right thumb and I looked unbelievingly at the blood spurting out. I did not believe this sort of thing could happen—'not to me'. Four tommygun bullets hit my left thigh.

Hours later, after a fire fight, I was taken prisoner, stripped and marched barefoot from halfway down South Korea to the North Korean capital. There, the brainwashing began. Twenty years passed before I could bring myself to write what happened in those brainwashing sessions.

They took me to where it all happened, at night and, when I left, I also left at night. The brainwashing room had pictures of Stalin, Mao and Kim II Sung on the walls, in colours that looked garish even in the constant penumbra of the room. There was a small table at which the brainwasher sat taking notes or consulting the dossier.

The room was quite large with windows on two sides, windows on which black paper had been pasted. There was one single bulb in a black cardboard cone which focused the light down

3

on the plain wooden chair in which I sat and on the front of the small table behind which sat my Russian brainwasher, whom I nicknamed Lavrenti after the head of Russia's police, Lavrenti P. Beria. Lavrenti himself was in the shadows. There were two other chairs in the shadows. There were two more chairs the assistants used and there usually was a brazier in which twigs were kept burning and from which the assistants of the team leader lit their cigarettes. I sat opposite Lavrenti, my hands no longer tied.[1]

The proceedings started amicably with Lavrenti inquiring about my wounds—the tommy-gun bullets in my leg had not gone deep at all and I had squeezed them out but the wounds were festering. He offered me a Russian cigarette and asked me to sit down. He spoke English with a very slight accent. He read from the dossier before him what my name was, who I worked for, where I had been caught. Then he stated that, according to my escorts, I had observed the bombing of several unarmed villages and saw women, children and old men killed by American planes.

I sat there and said nothing, looking at Lavrenti's hands which were the only part of him illuminated by the cone of light from the weak bulb. His fingers were like spatulas, wider at the ends. The nails were bitten to the flesh. There were no hairs growing on those fingers. They moved constantly: when he was not taking notes, he rolled small pieces of paper into spirals and made them bounce on the table.

Then, Lavrenti asked me to broadcast over the radio that I had seen American planes bomb unarmed villages. It was only the truth, he said, and it was a journalist's duty to tell the truth. I refused. I was resolved, at this point, not to do anything they asked. From what I had read of their procedures, the first concession by the victim always led to increased demands. What such demands could be I did not know precisely. It seemed likely, however, that they would try to extract from me all information I had. A journalist does not publish all he knows: often he is told things on an off-the-record basis. I did not know any state secrets of the West that the Kremlin might want but it was not unthinkable that I might know something which would confirm some information the Kremlin had. Most of all I feared that, once I gave in, I might eventually give away the names of people who—I knew—worked for the CIA or Britain's Intelligence Service. These were friends. Maybe the true nature of the work

4

of my friends was not known to the Kremlin. Maybe, if I was made to tell, these friends would lose their lives. I was convinced that, if I gave in once, I would lose all control over what I said: my one concession would be the thin end of the wedge.

Lavrenti had waited for me to talk and while he waited he leaned forward looking at me intently. I could see more of him now. He had thick black hair, prominent eyebrows, so prominent that they cast shadows on his eyes which were thus hidden. His nose was big, upturned and it shone in the light, the shine of a greasy skin. The nose cast a shadow which bisected his mouth and made its movements slightly grotesque.

He asked whether I approved of women and children being killed; whether I did not think it the responsibility of every man to prevent the killing of women and children. I said I was not a man because as a prisoner I had no free will and, therefore, had no responsibility. Without free will, without responsibility, I was not a man.

We had a very long amateurish philosophical discussion on free-will: a parody on Russia's nineteenth century literature.

Lavrenti sat forward, bending his head near the table so that only his hair was in the light. He had used brilliantine that smelled of rose water; the scent came to me through the strong smell of his cigarette. He was bouncing yet one more spiral of paper on the table. I could not see his eyes in the shadows, but I felt sure he was looking at me, studying me.

He began all over again, time after time, using the same phrases almost, repeating the same gestures, bouncing more and more paper spirals on the table, smoking cigarette after cigarette—not offering me any. His smell changed as more and more smoke permeated his hair. My mouth was getting drier, so dry that I felt tiny marbles of dry saliva on my tongue. I needed water but somehow I did not ask for a drink. It was my first bout with a brainwasher and, absurdly, I wanted to fight it on their terms. I too repeated the same answers each time Lavrenti posed the same questions over and over again.

Finally Lavrenti said that he might have misled the North Korean authorities in telling them they should take me for what I claimed I was. Maybe, he said, the North Koreans had been right all along about the view they had of me. I could not help asking what that view was.

Lavrenti did not bother to answer my question. He stood up and left the room with his two attendants. Two new attendants

5

immediately came in followed by a Mr Kim. He moved the table away from my chair and stood looking down at me. His head bumped the lampshade which swung for a while so that his image flickered from light to shadow. He wore a pale green short-sleeved shirt opened at the neck, wide, pleated, brown trousers and a soldier's black boots. His hair was black, very straight; he obviously tried to keep it plastered down without much success. His temples had been shaved. He was a tall man, quite handsome with a broad forehead, alert eyes, a good straight nose and a wide mouth over a firm chin. He looked more Eurasian than Korean and he spoke English with an Oxford accent. He told me, without my asking, that he had advanced degrees in ethnology and psychology. He wanted to know whether I was an important journalist. I said I was not.

How could I explain, then, Mr Kim asked, that an unimportant journalist like me had been the first to publish the story on how the Americans monitored Soviet nuclear tests? How could I explain that I had been the first to get the Grady letter which overthrew a Greek Government.[2] I tried to explain that I got those stories through a combination of luck and hard work—hard work, precisely because I was not yet important and I wanted to become important.

We played variations on this theme for endless hours. Finally Mr Kim asked whether I had been given those important stories as a payment for being an American spy. We went through a tennis match of affirmation and denial. I kept saying that Communist journalists might be spies but that I was not.

How then did I manage, Mr Kim asked, to infiltrate Albanian territory earlier in 1950? How did I manage to join up with Albanians who conspired against their own government in Albania? And why did I subsequently write 'criminal lies' about the Albanian government?

I felt sick. I had not told the interrogators about this story. I had sneaked into Albania and spent some days with remnants of the anti-Communist underground. And I had come out with a series of stories which had raised my stock as a journalist. That Mr Kim knew about this episode would make things difficult for me. By now he had pushed the table close to me and had sat down behind it, a Parker pen poised over a piece of paper.

The word 'spy', Mr Kim said, meant someone who stole information from a government.

6

I replied that journalists in the west constantly publish information their governments do not want published.

Mr Kim pointed out that I had not taken information from the government of my own country, but had entered another country to associate with its seditious elements. That was not 'good reporting', but spying. And did I know that the Geneva convention did not protect spies?

I shouted that I was not a spy, I had never been a spy and I would never have been stupid enough to work in such a dirty business as spying. I was only a journalist.

An unusual journalist, said Mr Kim: so-called journalist who operated clandestinely in another country; who was given choice stories by the Americans . . .

On and on and on, hour after hour, Mr Kim went over my whole story, asking the questions he had asked before and getting the same answers I had given before. He was making notes all the time while I could not make notes. I began wondering how soon, under the strain of sleeplessness, I would slip up, give an answer different from one I had previously given. It became terribly important to me that I should not slip. I could not even afford the luxury of being bored, in case I relaxed and said something that would help Kim in his arguments.

Eventually, Mr Kim left and a Mr Pak came in with two attendants. Mr Pak sat for a long time reading from my dossier which, by this time, contained notes made by Lavrenti and Kim. Every so often Mr Pak would look at me then he resumed reading the dossier.

I stood up to stretch and Mr Pak's attendants crashed me back onto the chair.

I said I wanted to go to the toilet. Mr Pak did not answer until I had asked three times. He motioned assent with his head and the guards took me out to a dirty toilet with no door. They stood there watching then escorted me back to the brainwashing room and sat me down roughly.

At that very instant, Mr Pak screamed: 'You are a spy'. He pushed away the table that separated us and brought his chair so close that our knees touched.

'You are a spy,' he repeated screaming still more loudly. 'You are a spy in the pay of the Americans. They sent you spying into Albania. They used you to make the Greek government fall. Only a spy of the Americans would know how Americans spy on Russian nuclear tests. You are a spy in the pay of the Amer-

7

icans. They sent you spying into Albania. They used you to make the Greek government fall. Only a spy of the Americans would know how Americans spy on Russian nuclear tests . . .' The refrain is inscribed indelibly in my memory.

He went on repeating the same text, screaming so loudly that the veins stood out on his neck. I kept saying 'no' to each segment of his accusation. My head felt as if it would explode. My eyes burned, my neck ached so that I could hardly keep my head up. But Mr Pak was indefatigable. His screaming went on, at the same pitch. His head was tilted back and the light from the lamp bathed his face. It seemed incongruous that so small a face could produce so much noise. His face appeared smaller than it really was, perhaps, because his shoulders were so broad and he had the neck muscles of a wrestler.

A different voice said that I looked terrible. The voice came from very far. I tried to focus my eyes. Lavrenti was back, behind the desk.

He remarked that the wounds on my leg looked bad and that he could smell the pus.

The 'barbarous' American raids, said Lavrenti, had killed many Korean doctors. Those who were left were working day and night. There was an established list of priorities on the basis of which, doctors' services were allocated and I was not on the priority list because his Korean friends were convinced that I was a spy and spies were generally executed, not given medical treatment.

The execution scene flashed before my eyes: I was being led out into a courtyard and placed against a wall. I was given a cigarette which I smoked. I refused to be blindfolded. Then the commands to the firing squad. Would one of them have a blank cartridge so that each of the twelve executioners might be able to tell himself he had not participated in the killing? I was smiling as the officer commanding the squad raised his sword. In what film had I seen this scene? I said that if they executed me, they would be executing an innocent journalist, that killing me would be murder for no reason; that they would be held accountable before world opinion.

I was not that important, said Lavrenti. World opinion would not really be aroused by my death.

I was a journalist, I said. Other journalists would make a fuss about me, even if they did not know me. They would keep asking what happened to me. I was an editor in my imagination, on

8

The Times, shaking my head over a small editorial accusing the Communists of barbarously executing an innocent journalist. I leaned back in my editorial chair, looked at my panelled walls with pictures of my predecessors. Then I looked at the young man who had brought in the copy. Reluctantly, I gave it back to him. No, we could not run an editorial on Deane again. Shame he was killed but he was a dead story.

Other journalists would not keep asking for long, said Lavrenti. They could be told I had confessed to being a spy and they could be given a tape of my confession in my own voice.

I answered that everyone knew a tape-recording can be edited. Lavrenti laughed : no one knew I was still alive, he said. There were witnesses, I pointed out; there were American soldiers with me when I was caught who would eventually say I was still alive.

I regretted those words, the minute I had spoken them. Those American soldiers, if questioned by the Koreans, could also say that, though a civilian, in civilian clothes, I had fought. The thought scared me badly because I believed that the Geneva convention did not protect someone who wore civilian clothes but who fought nevertheless.

Maybe these American soldiers were killed by American bombs after they were caught. At that instant, as if on cue, the sirens sounded.

They were going to the air raid shelter, Lavrenti said. They would lock me in the room. Maybe the question of my death would be determined quite soon.

I heard the sound of the key turning in the door and I was left alone. Soon the sound of anti-aircraft guns began rattling the house. Then there was the answering roar of bombs. I reviewed the conversation I had had with Lavrenti. He did not accuse me of having fought though dressed in civilian clothes. Did this mean that the American soldiers had not said anything? I could not be sure and my anxiety on this point was rising : my fear of what the American soldiers might say was to haunt me through the one thousand days of my captivity.

The bombs fell ever nearer. The walls shook. I could not abandon myself to fear. What if they were watching me? I had thought of lying down under the table : if the roof caved in because of a near miss, the table might prevent my being killed by falling rafters. But if they were watching me, or if they came back suddenly, they would know I had given in to fear.

9

No, I must not show fear. I stood up, put my left leg on the table and looked at my wounds. The four holes made by the tommy-gun bullets were full of pus. What could I do? Gritting my teeth, I squeezed around each hole till I could make no more pus come out but only blood. Then I went to the brazier and picked up some twigs that were not entirely burnt. Holding the unburnt end, I plunged the burning end of a twig in each of the four holes. The smell of burning flesh filled the room. I was not sure that this sort of cauterisation would help. I had dim memories of having read a story about such methods being used before the invention of antiseptics. Then I packed the holes with ash from the brazier—that should be disinfected, at least. Finally, I tore one sleeve off the shirt the Koreans had given me and bound my leg. Just as I was finishing, the all clear sounded and Lavrenti walked in again.

He took in the scene—pus on his table, the twigs, the smell of burning flesh, the torn shirt, the rough bandage. I would not be needing a doctor, he said. I might have so aggravated my condition that I would die of the wounds I suffered at the front.

I thought: he is trying to impress me with the fact that they do not care whether I live or die. I must not show fear.

'We were discussing the question of your death,' Lavrenti said. 'Actually, you are already dead. We heard an American radio broadcast that said you were presumed to have been killed. I am sorry you could not have heard the broadcast your-self, the radio in this room does not work.'

Then I noticed for the first time in the darkest corner—to which Lavrenti was pointing—an ancient looking radio receiver.

What did I think would be the reaction of my relatives to the announcement of my death, Lavrenti asked. If they got no news, they would feel anguish in the uncertainty. My father, a seasoned soldier, would know how to bear the news of my death; but my mother . . . My wife was young, was she young enough to quickly get over losing me? How quickly? I wonder? How long would it take her to forget me? Or rather, how long before she needed a man?

This is a new tack he is taking, I told myself, trying to see the expression on Lavrenti's face—but he was leaning back and was in the shadows. His hands were still: he was not playing with his paper springs. And his voice had a clinical character.

The longer I remained a prisoner, Lavrenti said, the more I would believe my wife had a lover. I would come out full of

10

complexes. I would expect her to wipe the slate clean and accept my clumsy sexual efforts. And I would be clumsy because I would be out of practice . . .

Eventually Lavrenti stood up abruptly and left the room. Pak succeeded him. I had hoped it would be Kim.

Kim came later. Then Pak again. And Lavrenti. They all said the same thing in their particular styles: that if they won quickly by throwing the Americans into the sea, they would have no accounts to give. They would not have to account for me. They could keep me till they made sure I could not harm the world Communist movement. If the war dragged on, I might be prisoner a long time, unless I gave them proof I was not an enemy of the people:

'And if you lose the war?'

Then, they said, neither I nor they would be alive to talk about it. If I co-operated with them, they would set me free. I would be able to rejoin my wife almost immediately. If I did not co-operate, then they would have to think of me as an enemy and I would either stay there a very long time or for ever.

'What do you mean by co-operation?' I knew what the answer would be so I was not concentrating. I drifted off into thoughts that preceded sleep. I thought of my father and my uncle Yanis in court, when they were being tried for their lives in 1935 after taking part in an unsuccessful coup to overthrow a fascist government. Uncle Yanis had often slept in the dock, bored by the proceedings. When they were asked by their lawyers to take the stand and plead for mercy, father refused. Uncle Yanis took the stand, polished his monocle, screwed it into his eye and said: 'If I had the opportunity, I would rebel against this government again.'

I saw the president of the tribunal, in his military uniform with the black flashes of the artillery officer on his collar. He was reading the sentences of father and uncle Yanis: 'The tribunal finds you guilty of treason. You will be put to death by firing squad.' Uncle Yanis yawned.

I too yawned as I was lifted back into my chair by the guards: I had fallen asleep and off the chair. One of them took my chin in his right hand and shook my head from side to side.

The guard was still shaking my head. I tried to speak but it was difficult to speak while he held my chin.

How long the sessions went on, I cannot tell. I was being held upright in my chair by the guards most of the time. Occasionally they would shake my head by the chin. At other times, one guard would hold my head, keeping my eyes open with his thumbs and forefingers. Mr Pak, when he was on duty, screamed as he had during his first session with me.

The guards continued to keep me from sleeping. The point came when even by holding my eyelids apart they could not keep me awake. I knew when I fell asleep and for a while I heard myself snoring. A searing pain woke me. My right arm had been twisted behind my back and the wrist was being bent. The pressure stopped just short of dislocation.

'I am not going to scream,' I told myself. 'I am not going to scream. I am not. I am not.' But Mr Pak was screaming. I remember wondering how it was that he did not lose his voice. He screamed, this time, with his face practically touching mine. I smelled the stench of fermented soya bean paste: 'You will never get out of here if you do not co-operate. You will never get out of here. Your wife will sleep with men. She will find one she will like better than you. You will never get out of here. Your wife will find one man she will like better than you. You will never get . . .'

That was when it first happened: I split into two. I was there in the chair awake, being screamed at, with my wrist nearly breaking but I was feeling no pain, I was not smelling Mr Pak's mildewy breath and my ears were hearing nothing: and I was also soaring out of the chair but watching that chair. My self which was not in the chair became a small boy, not quite twelve, in his apartment in Athens on the day before which my father and my uncle were to go through the ceremony of degradation à la Dreyfus before being executed for their anti-fascist coup.

There were fists pounding on the apartment door. I was alone. Mother was out on her endless round of seeking audiences with fascist notables to plead for father's life. I opened the door. Three policemen came in.

I had been told they would come to take father's beautiful sword, the sword of honour given him in 1916 with his first decoration, the highest Greek decoration for bravery. They were going to file through the sword so that it would have a weak point and could be broken over the knee, during the degradation. 'Ah,' said the maid, 'if only you knew how your father won that sword.'

She settled down comfortably on the sofa and I, nine years old now, lay with my head on her plump thigh, with her big breasts hanging over me, stretching her thin cotton dress. She smelled of scented soap and of another smell I did not know but which I always liked.

'Tell me,' I asked, turning my head so that I faced her belly. She had told me the story many times. So had others. It was a famous story in Greece. I breathed deeply and relaxed. Soon she would be putting me into my cold bed and I wanted the session on the sofa prolonged. 'It was a dreadful battle,' she said. My eyes closed, I could visualise the successive expressions on her face—there was always the same succession of expressions when she told that story, living it with her huge black eyes and her enormous mouth that bisected her olive skin.

'There was this hill the Germans were holding in Macedonia. They had dug inside it.' Her hands made digging motions on my belly while I wriggled with pleasure. 'And they had machine guns sticking out firing, ack—ack—ack.' Her fingers outstretched, kept time with the ack—ack—ack, recoiling like gun barrels then moving back into position. 'For days, the French and the English tried to take the hill. They bombarded it with big cannons, broum, broum, broum.' She fashioned explosion shapes in the air. 'But they could not take it. They would get half-way up, and then they would retreat.'

This was the point at which I always asked: 'And then?'

'Ah, and then! Then your father—he was only nineteen, but the most beautiful officer in the army, volunteered to try. "No! No!" said his friends. "No Lakis! You will be killed!" And he laughed showing his beautiful teeth. "No, I won't. Nobody can kill me today!" He knew the Virgin Mary, the leader of Greek armies, was going to shield him.'

'How did he know?'

'Your father knows everything,' said the maid, fondling me. 'And he was right, because he didn't die. Now that proves he knew, doesn't it? So he asked for volunteers and all the soldiers wanted to follow him.'

'Why?'

'Because they could see the light around him, the light of the Virgin Mary who was going to shield them. But he didn't take all the soldiers. He chose them carefully. He took burglars, and poachers and chicken thieves and stealers of sheep. Oh, he knew what he was doing. And he made them cover their clothes and faces and hands with mud.'

13

'Why?' I asked, waiting breathlessly for the answer I knew so well.

'Because they were going to take the hill at night. Now the night was never dark over that hill because the enemy was firing things that lit up the sky. But your father had studied the hill and had made a picture of it in his mind. There were parts of the hill that stayed in the shadows always, and it was that way your father led his men.'

She was getting warmer with the telling of the story and the smells that came from her were doing strange things to me.

'What else did he do?' I asked dreamily.

'Ah, what else did he do? He had watched the hill night after night and he knew that the Germans fired their machine guns every now and then, just to make sure that nobody would get up the hill in the dark. Your father figured out exactly how the machine guns fired: now to the left, now to the right. So he started up the hill and he managed to keep his men in the shadows and out of the machine-gun bullets, most of the time but then . . .'

I had sat up and was looking at her face: I always looked at her at this point. Perspiration was beaded on her forehead. Her eyes were dilated in horror.

'What happened then?' I asked panting to hear what I knew was coming.

'Then the dirty Germans began firing their guns differently and a bullet hit your father. It hit his helmet and dazed him; he fell; another bullet hit his hand, breaking his finger. His soldiers thought he was dead. They raised a great cry. "Gigantes is dead!" And he heard them, shook his head, bit off his broken finger, stood up and yelled: "Follow me, boys! We'll get the dirty dogs!" And he ran up the hill alone, and no bullet hit him because the Virgin Mary was with him. And he threw a grenade into an enemy machine-gun post, and it blew up. And his men, roaring like lions, ran after him, and the Virgin Mary protected them too and they took the hill. And the next day the French general and the English general gave your father medals. And the Greek prime minister gave him the highest medal and a beautiful sword. And all the girls ran after your father.'

I was nearly twelve again and the policeman wanted the sword. Father had told them he kept it in the hall cupboard but they couldn't find it. I could have answered I did not know but I said I hid it. And so I had my first police beating. They hit my head and I remember the taste of blood at the back of my nose. For a while, they stopped hitting and twisted one of my arms, bending the wrist to dislocation. One can see pain of this kind. It is red to start, a red cocoon. It turns to whorls of paling orange, followed by yellow shooting stars and a final white sunburst—all in the rear of the eyes—as tendons give and the hand hangs limp. Then they began hitting me again and I do not know for how long because I was left unconscious to be revived by my mother's anguished screaming.

But I really woke to the screaming of Mr Pak and my two selves were one again and I was in the chair having my hand twisted by the guards, while Mr Pak screamed on and on and on. Through the pain I noticed his refrain had changed somewhat.

'The capitalist radio says you are dead. Nobody knows you are alive. Your wife thinks you are dead. She will find a man to sleep with her. The capitalist radio says . . .'

The air raid alarm sounded. Bombs fell near and shook the house. Pak and the guards left me alone. The pain in my wrist ebbed and I fought against sleep. I kept saying to myself over and over again that according to the capitalist radio I was dead. Finally the full meaning of these words seemed to galvanise me. Oblivious of my fatigue, I rose and went to the radio which they had said was broken. It was plugged in. I switched it on but nothing happened. I roamed and found there were three radio sets in the house, none of which appeared to work. By changing some of the tubes around, I got one of the sets functioning and I turned it to the American Forces Network.

'And now the baseball scores' : the voice was unmistakably American. Then there was music : *If I knew you were coming I'd have baked a cake* and *Put another nickel in the Nickelodeon, all I want is loving you and music.*

Lavrenti came in, while bombs were still falling. I switched off the radio the minute I heard the door but I had been too late.

So I could repair broken radios too. How did I think Lavrenti's Korean friends would interpret this? Already Lavrenti had great difficulties in convincing them I was not a spy, he said. Now I gave proof of knowing about radio equipment . . .

He was standing under the light but his nose was not shining. I remember wondering whether he had just washed. I did not say anything.

15

The Koreans were also talking about my endurance, Lavrenti said. They thought I had been pre-conditioned, as spies are. Pre-conditioning was administered so the spy would not break down immediately. This gave his side two or three days to protect their operations from the consequences of his breaking down. But 'my' side did not think. I had been captured: they had announced I was dead. Slowly, monotonously Lavrenti began again from the beginning, testing to see, as he said, what it was that I reacted to most strongly. I fell asleep.

Then I was drowning. I was four years old and I was drowning. Father had taken me in a rowboat and pulled away from shore where mother, for some reason, was crying. He was smiling, wearing his black bathing suit, his skin pale and white, except for the big livid scar where the shrapnel had hit him and nearly killed him in 1917. He was talking to me but I was not paying attention. I was interested in the structure of the boat and in the small dead fish which sloshed in the bilge water, under the duck-boards.

Father stopped rowing. He picked me up and threw me into the water. I felt for the sand with my feet but there wasn't any and I went down. Water went up my nostrils and I panicked. I thrashed with my arms and my legs and broke to the surface where I gulped air before going down again. Next time I surfaced, I stayed up longer, long enough to see father at the edge of the boat, smiling and clicking his teeth together, as he always did, to show approval.

'Move your arms like this,' I heard, and went down again. I came up doing a frantic dog paddle, trying to reach the boat: father lazily rowed it out of reach. I went down again, tired and frightened and I felt his hand pulling me out and into the boat.

'If you don't stop crying,' he said, 'I'll hit you. You know now you can float. So in you go again.' He threw me. The water hit my face first.

'Mr Deane,' said Lavrenti, 'next time you fall asleep, I shall let the guards twist your arm instead of throwing water on you. You can surely stay awake.' But I could not and my wrist was again being bent and I was telling myself I would not scream.

I spent a great deal of time in dissociation. Once, I was four again on the island of which father was the military governor. It had an old Venetian lighthouse which could be reached by a disused staircase, up a cliff. I climbed it. Father and uncle Yanis stood at the bottom not daring to shout for fear of so diverting

16

my attention that I would lose my footing. When I came down, they took turns beating me. I said I was sorry and the beating increased. I sobbed.

'If you want the beating to stop,' father said, 'you will stop crying.'

'Please stop,' I said. Uncle Yanis' strap hit me harder than before.

'You do not plead,' said uncle Yanis. 'You are a Gigantes.'

On another occasion I was off again with uncle Yanis. His sentence of death had been commuted to life imprisonment and then to exile; eventually he came back to Greece and I was with him, a teenager.

He was wearing his favourite pepper and salt tweeds, a striped shirt with a white starched collar and highly polished shoes. He was discoursing on being best, *aien aristeuein*, the motto Hector spoke before he went out to be killed by Achilles.

'You must be best,' uncle Yanis said; and he added with obvious satisfaction, 'I have always been best.'

'Better than father?'

'As a fighter I was as good as he was. He cared about that. He was best when he cared to be, but there were things he did not care about, and then he was not best.' Uncle Yanis spoke with love about his brother but also with disappointment. 'He could have been best at everything.'

'But why be best at everything?'

'Why be best at everything? That is the only thing in life. The only true joy.'

He had already spoken about the subject and his methods and they always involved pain. I did not like pain.

'If you want to be a champion runner,' uncle Yanis said, 'you tell your heart, your lungs and your feet what to do: literally, you tell them. You say to your heart, "beat as fast as you like, I don't care". And you tell your lungs, "you won't burst because I don't allow you". Your feet will be the worst. You will keep putting them down one after the other and they will hurt more and more. And they will talk back at you. But you must not listen. And you know how you do that? By concentrating on the pain, by studying it. After a while, it is not your pain you are observing but a pain external to yourself.'

Uncle Yanis removed the filter from his Dunhill cigarette holder, inserted a new one, lit a cigarette and walked silently for a while, watching the undulating buttocks of a young woman who had emerged ahead of us from a side street. She entered a house.

'Ah yes,' said uncle Yanis, 'that was nice. Have I told you how I stopped being a morphine addict?' My jaw fell open. Uncle Yanis a drug addict?

'You heard about my wound in the Great War? An artillery shell exploded before me in the Great War. They told me later that my remains looked like a corpse on which buzzards had been feasting.' He stopped and looked at his reflection in a shop window as if he could hardly believe he was there. 'I am still beautifully built,' he said with satisfaction.

'My soldiers picked up my remains,' he continued 'and brought them back in a blanket. The doctors told me later they had been amazed to see I was still alive. I spent two years in plaster or on the operating table. They rebuilt me and, of course, they kept me full of morphia. When I finally came out of the plaster I was a morphia addict.'

He told me about his first realisation that he was an addict, the cramps, the irresistible craving, the trembling race to a friendly doctor who injected him with a light dose.

'I stopped trembling. I heard the doctor telling me I was an addict. I answered I would stop being an addict as from that moment. I talked the doctor into giving me one more dose. He smiled with pity as he gave me the packet of powder. I took the dose to my room, put it on the table and waited for the next withdrawal pains. I picked up the morphia and held it in my hands but did not take it. I cried; I shook; but I did not take the morphia. This went on for months. I never threw the morphia dose away. I beat the habit. Do you know how? By concentrating on the pains, and the cramps, by studying them, cherishing them, till I actually missed them. . .'

Then I would be seven years old in Paris, arriving at my French school without knowing a word of French. That night father, who was in Paris studying at the Staff College, sat up with me making me memorise the homework phonetically. At the end of the first term he came to parents' day. The school mistress was complimentary.

'For a little lad from the Middle East, he has done splendidly. He stands fifth in the class. Really, I am amazed, considering . . .'

Father walked me home and as soon as we were in he began slapping my face from side to side.

'From the Middle East, are you? A little Arab, are you?' he

18

asked punctuating his questions with slaps. 'You are a Gigantes, aren't you? You will be first, do you hear?'

Then there was the fighting. My school in Paris, the Lycée Janson de Sailly, had a lot of royalists. We Gigantes were anti-monarchists. They held me down, squeezing my throat, telling me to shout 'long live the king'. A teacher pulled them off me.

'What are these marks on your throat?' father asked. I told him. Had I beaten those boys? No, I had not. Father slapped my face, palm, backhand, palm, backhand.

'That's for letting them beat a Gigantes. Now get them one by one and beat them.'

I did but I was caught doing it and received zero for conduct.

'You let yourself be caught? They did not tell on you? You were just caught?' Slaps punctuated the questions. That night he came to kiss me good night and stayed to tell me the story of the Spartan boy who stole a fox cub: he hid the cub under his tunic and rather than admit to the theft, let the animal eat his entrails.

Mr Pak was punching me in the stomach. I was back in the chair. I had spat in his face. The guards were holding me and he was punching me in the stomach, screaming: 'You will never get out. You will be executed, dirty capitalist spy. You will never get out. You . . .'

Lavrenti came in and said that my behaviour showed I was a well pre-conditioned individual. Only professionals have such conditioning. He would not be able to convince his Korean friends that they should not shoot me.

The sirens sounded and Lavrenti left. I noticed that they had taken the radio away and that this time they did not bother to lock the door. Then I lay on the floor and fell asleep. Lavrenti woke me to talk about my wife. He was a psychiatrist, he said, and had treated couples split by the war: He told me the story of Boris and Natasha his wife. Boris was a naval officer, married less than two years when his ship was sunk and he was taken captive by the Germans . . .

Lavrenti fancied himself as a story teller: on and on he talked, in the worst cheap magazine style giving every detail of Natasha's easy seduction by various men after her husband was taken prisoner by the Germans.

Then he turned explicitly pornographic, describing in the crudest words what Natasha did with her lovers. It was badly told but the repetitiousness was overwhelming.

19

'I want to go to the toilet,' I said to Lavrenti. 'I must go now. I can't hold myself.'

The foul smelling excrement poured out of me; it came in waves and flowed from my clothes onto the floor. Hastily, Lavrenti left the room and the guards, swearing, making noises of disgust, pounced on me. They dragged me out into the courtyard and made me remove my clothes which they threw into the outdoor privy. Then they made me fetch water from a pump, made me wash myself and took me back to the room with pail and rags, to clean the floor. As I was kneeling, cleaning my own filth, one of the guards grabbed my hair and pushed my face into the filth. As if I were a puppy being house trained, I had my nose rubbed in the dirt and, at that moment, I was two again : on the floor, in my degradation and also soaring watching another degradation.

I had skipped school on the day father and uncle Yanis and their companions were to be publicly stripped of their rank. I wanted to see. The parade ground of the military school was ringed by a mob, men, some women too, who had sacks of stone, rotten eggs and even of excrement.

A sergeant of the gendarmerie ripped off father's buttons, the insignia of rank, his ribbons, the coloured testimonials of the blood he had shed for the country, so many times. Then the swords of the condemned men were broken. Only father's sword was not there to be broken. Finally, by obvious pre-arrangement, the mob broke ranks and began throwing stones and rotten eggs. One man had a thin, pale face with black circles under his eyes, a small moustache carefully trimmed over thick sensuous lips, ears that stood out from plastered mousy hair and a nervous chin bouncing on a large adam's apple which bobbed in and out of a greasy collar. His shoulders were narrow, a narrowness unhidden by the padding in the coat. His baggy trousers ended inches above the ground showing rayon socks covered in gaudy flowers so that the shoes looked like flower pots that had gone wrong in the potter's kiln. With unblinking eyes I watched this little man standing in flowered socks, moustache contorted in a sort of glee, eyes half closed with pleasure. He slapped my father's face, then, digging a carefully manicured hand into a paper sack, brought out a handful of excrement and rubbed it into the new bruise.

I stood waiting for my father to show a sign of emotion. I prayed for him to look hurt, to cry so that I too could cry :

20

because he didn't, I could not, though I wanted to

On the floor, on my hands and knees, my face rubbed in filth by the guard, I said nothing, even when they kicked me while I cleaned the floor. They made me fetch water three times before they felt the floor and my chair were clean enough. Though the pail was heavy, I enjoyed the trips to the courtyard. We were on a slight rise and below us ran the river Taedong. There was a flagpole in the courtyard with a rope but no flag. I wondered if this had been a consulate or some foreign mission. There was much debris too, a piece of copper pipe, a red rag, a length of bamboo. I was noticing these things particularly though I was not quite sure why. On the river bank, not far below, driftwood had been washed ashore.

They marched me in again, sat me on the chair and gave me a piece of faded black cloth to put around my middle before they called Lavrenti back into the room.

He said that the room still smelled and proceeded to discuss my inability to control my orifices. It was not dysentery, he said, but a loss of emotional control because I couldn't bear the thought that my wife was behaving the way Natasha, Boris's wife had behaved. I said something like: 'If you want to think that your tales of Boris and Natasha make me want to crap, go ahead—it's pretty shitty stuff, your story.' He kept up the clinically pornographic descriptions with the same effect on my bowels.

An end was finally put to the pornography when the air raid warning sounded and Lavrenti left for the shelter without locking the door. I presume they left me unguarded, in a room they did not lock, because they thought me too weakened to move far.

I sat still in my chair for a few moments, waiting for the wail to stop. When the sirens fell quiet I stood up. I had felt exhausted only a few moments before but now my exhaustion seemed to have vanished. I went to the door and walked down the corridor to the outer door. It too was unlocked. Outside, the darkness of the night was slashed by searchlight beams. I went out into the courtyard, picked up the piece of copper pipe I had seen earlier, took the length of bamboo, the red rag and finally detached the halyard from the flagpole. Then I made for the river Taedong, at the bottom of the slope. There I inspected the driftwood. I tied myself to the trunk that seemed the least waterlogged and dragged it into the river. The bottom was slimy and I slipped often, but finally I was in deep enough water for the current to catch the log. I had secured the copper pipe, the length of bamboo and the red rag to the trunk with one end of the rope I had, and I shortened the loop at the other end which connected me to the trunk.

I was floating down the river. I felt giddy with triumph. They would not suspect I would take that route to escape. They would have to think I was mad. But I was not mad. I was a navigator and I remembered from my navy days that the tides in the Gulf of Korea where the Taedong flowed, were among the strongest in the world. With luck, I would be able to land at night, steal some form of food, a receptacle for water; with luck I might reach the estuary, hiding in bulrushes till the night tide and then I could be taken miles out to sea. I had a red rag and a bamboo pole so I could signal. American ships would be patrolling the Gulf of Korea constantly. One might see me. What were my chances, I asked myself and immediately decided not to try such a calculation. It was enough that I was out of the house, free, floating towards the sea. My rope seemed in good enough condition and it was still summer—the water was not too cold. I nearly lost the black piece of cloth they had given me to replace my soiled clothes and so I tied the cloth around me like a breech clout.

How far had I gone? It was a clear night and I could see the stars. The Big Dipper stood out and I found Polaris. I seemed to be floating south and a little to the west. I could detect no signs of the dawn to the east but I did not know what time it could be. How soon should I look for a safe hiding place for the daylight hours? What if I waited too long and found none when dawn came? That was a chance I would have to take: I had to get as far as possible while it was dark. Floating down the river, submerged through the daylight hours and breathing through the copper pipe, would be too risky, since I would not be able to see possible hazards. The pipe could only serve for brief emergencies.

My log hit a mudbank. I had gone too close to shore. I tried to get back into the stream and the fatigue of the previous days (how many had there been?) engulfed me. I stood on the mudbank, tugging at the log and felt myself sinking to my knees. Then I fell flat on my face and choked as I breathed water. I raised myself in a panic, coughing and retching. Was there anyone near there to hear me? I forced myself to stop coughing and listened with my heart pounding in my chest. There were sounds. The air raid had stopped. I could hear no explosions. I could hear dogs, though, and once I heard a man's voice far away.

I stood up again and tugged once more at the log. It was no use. It seemed stuck firmly in the mudbank. Feeling along the log with my hands I found that one of its branches was stuck into the bank. I had been pulling in the wrong direction, sinking the branch deeper into the mud. I changed the direction of my pull. It was slow work: I had to rest every few seconds. Finally I was adrift again, clinging to the log. I had disarranged the rope during my efforts to get free of the mudbank and it was not supporting me—I had to hold on to the log by my hands and I was finding this hard. Holding on with one hand, I worked to arrange the rope so that my head would be kept out of the water without my having to expend any effort. I am right-handed and my right thumb had a bullet in it, so it was with the left hand and my teeth that I was trying to make a proper bowline. By the time I completed that task, I noticed a slight fading of the stars: Polaris was only just visible. To the East, I could see pink. This was the emergency I had feared. Where would I hide? I began looking but I could not see very far because only my head protruded from the water. I lifted myself onto the log to get a better vantage point but it was still too dark to distinguish much. I did not dare try to steer for shore because I did not know what I would find there.

My problem was solved by the river itself. It began curving a little more to the west and, in the turn, the current resisted all my feeble efforts to steer. Soon my log was caught in a tangle of driftwood clustered around a tiny island very close to the shore.

Should I free my log and continue downstream? I tried to see as much as I could of the shore but to no avail: the bank was several feet high and I was close enough to it so as not to be able to see what lay beyond. My indecision went when I heard voices and I saw the bow of a boat creeping out from behind a point upstream. I dived under and hid among the driftwood. The boat came very near. It contained an old man and a boy.

I thought back: for how long had I heard the voices before I saw the boat? Had the voices sounded as if they had been stationary—had the old man and the boy been on shore when they had spoken and then had entered the boat? Yes, that was it: they had been on shore, quite near, standing there, speaking,

23

before taking to the water. So there was a house nearby and that represented risk. I was close enough to the shore for anyone to see me from the bank. On the other hand, the occupants of the boat had passed very close but had not seen me. I decided I had better use what remained of the semi-darkness to make myself some sort of driftwood screen on the tiny island so that I could lie there till night. There was enough small driftwood among the big pieces and soon I had a sort of beaver's tangle under which I lay.

Day came and, with it, the noises from the bank increased. I tried to keep awake, to anticipate possible dangers, but sleep overcame me. It did not last long. The sun was still low in the eastern sky when the barking of a dog startled me. He was a big dog with a strong strain of German shepherd, unless it was a wolf. He stood on the shore looking down at me and barking. A good guard dog. Soon a woman appeared. She did not look in my direction : she just kicked the dog and he followed her whimpering.

I kept drifting in and out of sleep. The dog kept coming back; I was sure he was barking at me. I do not remember any of my dreams. I do remember my thoughts. They were giddy thoughts of freedom. In my mind, I was finding equally good hiding places each dawn, places to land at night where I could steal food and maybe a bottle against the time when I might need fresh water at sea. I thought of the grey, graceful shape of the destroyer that would pick me out of the water and the thought was so vivid that in my mind I was already free, with a lump in my throat at the kindness my rescuers would show me. There would be a steak, and ice-cream, good coffee, clean clothes, a bed and merciful safe sleep while the ship's radio announced my sensational escape.

On that little island, I did not think at all of what had gone on in the brainwashing house and my thoughts of freedom did not go beyond the day after my rescue, when I would sit at a typewriter to be a reporter again.

A dead fish floated down stream and stuck among the driftwood surrounding me. I lay a few feet from the dead fish pondering whether I should risk eating it. Hunger cramps were twisting my belly but could I risk ptomaine poisoning? Would I risk poisoning, though? How decomposed did a fish have to be before it could give ptomaine poisoning? I realised how insufficient my knowledge of such things was and decided that before my next assignment I would try to find out. I fell asleep wondering why I thought I might need to know, ever again, how safe decomposing fish were to eat.

Thirst woke me. I crawled out of my tangle of driftwood to the water's edge and lapped at the water. Something touched my nose. It was the decomposing fish. I picked it up and crawled back hastily into my shelter because the watch dog was back calling attention to me once more.

If I had drunk the water so near the fish, I said to myself, then I must have already contracted any of the things I could catch from eating it. I paused and asked myself whether this was really so, but I paused very briefly. I peeled the skin, removed the head and the tail and squeezed along its back and abdomen. The flesh came off the spinal column. I threw away the entrails and took the first mouthful. The smell was definitely worse than the taste. I gulped down the fish without chewing and then crept back to the water to wash the smell from my mouth and my hands. The dog did not interrupt me this time but I heard the boat returning and I was afraid to move. I lay there, in the open, staring at the old man and the boy in the boat. More than once I was sure they were looking at me. I saw their eyes and was sure they must have seen me. Then I realised that the sun was low and that the shadows from my driftwood shelter were criss crossing all over my body. I was between the boat and the sun. They could not possibly have seen me, I told myself. But could I be sure? Might they not have pretended not to have seen me so that I would stay where I was and be easy to find? What should I do? My impulse was to begin drifting downstream at once but it was not dark enough and the risk of my being seen, especially as I tried to disengage my log, would be too great. Anxiously, I waited till total darkness. I took time to make sure I was secured to the log as comfortably as possible, that my tube, my bamboo pole and my rag were secure and then I cast adrift. I had tied myself so that even if I fell asleep, my head would not go under water.

I did not fall asleep, even though I was exhausted: a motor boat passed me, circled me, went upstream then came towards me again. Was it looking for me? It had no lights so how could it be looking for me? But then what would a motor boat be doing at night, in total darkness on the Taedong river? It was now almost upon me. Frantically I worked on my bowline to loosen it so I could duck my head under water, but before the knot came loose, I was ridden under by the motor boat. The keel grazed my head. Then there was a grinding noise as the propeller bit into the trunk.

My lungs were bursting when I surfaced. The occupants of the boat, some yards away, were engaged in violent argument. The motor died—someone had switched it off. Then there was the sound of oars squealing against oarlocks. The boat made for the shore and I continued drifting, madly excited again with thoughts of freedom. They could not have been looking for me. But what had they been doing? I gave up searching for an answer to that question because there was another bump, a bump into something soft. A vagary of the river current had brought my log into collision with a floating corpse, a female corpse, as I could see by the light of the moon. One breast was still there, uppermost. The other was gone. Eaten by buzzards? Blown up in an explosion? Soon there were more corpses around me and the remains of a boat—a stanchion, a piece of stern. So this was what the motor boat was doing: searching the river for possible survivors. Maybe a bomb had hit a ferry boat. That meant there would be more searching down the river.

I was drifting downstream with my macabre companions, lacerated, drawn and quartered. A torso floated face down; it must have belonged to a man before. I had to part company with them. If I went on downstream with them, I would surely be found and caught. I had to stop moving. Doing the breast stroke across a current, dragging a driftwood log behind took what energy I had left. Finally I touched bottom. The shore, not far away, rose naked and steep.

For some time I walked slowly, chest high in water, along the shore dragging my log in search of my next hiding place. I found one, another islet besieged by driftwood. I changed the position of the rope on my log, making the knot under water, around the branch that had stuck earlier in the mudbank. Then I built myself another driftwood tangle. My rate of progress was excessively slow: numbed by fatigue, I had almost no strength left. As the pink light of dawn crept up the sky from the east, I heard a bump against the logs. It was not the sound of wood on wood. Slowly, I crept towards the noise and found myself face to face with another corpse. This one would give me away. I went into the water and tried to drag the corpse under the logs. It must have taken the best part of an hour—the whole sky was light by the time the corpse was submerged and fastened with my rope so that it stayed under water. When the last knot was tied I heard the sounds of another boat. I took a deep breath and dived under searching for my copper tube. I stayed under water, breathing through the tube. The current, passed unevenly through the logs, giving a pulsing movement to the corpse's limbs which nudged me rhythmically. I did not know when it would be safe to raise my head. Had the boat gone? I tried to see but the logs around me obscured my view. I tried to listen to the sounds of a boat—water carries sound well. But the current passing through the logs made too much noise. All I could tell was that up there, beyond the surface of the water, there was light.

And then I panicked because I fell momentarily asleep, my lips grew slack on the copper tube and I breathed water. By some reflex I was still holding onto the tube, I resisted the temptation to surface and coughed holding the tube to my mouth. Then I began breathing again.

How not to fall asleep once more? I made myself change the hand that held the tube. I opened my eyes wide and rolled them. I curled and uncurled my toes. But sleep kept creeping up on me. Finally I jammed my wounded thumb between two logs that were tightly held together by the current. They never came apart but the current made them pulsate against one another. The result, for me, was a succession of blows on the thumb whose top joint was traversed by a bullet from a Russian tommy-gun. The bullet had not severed the nerve. Each blow on the wound seared through me and was enough to keep me awake. The two logs I was using were so positioned that I would have felt even more pain had I tried inadvertently to pull out my thumb.

Thus ended the day. In the darkness, I released the corpse and let it float on its way. Then I made for the shore. Hunger was again gripping my stomach. There had been no dead fish this day. Climbing the four foot bank proved impossible. I did not have the strength. I moved upstream, searching for a lower bank: if I had to beat a hasty retreat to my islet and my hideaway of driftwood, going downstream would be quicker.

Eventually I came upon a tiny sandy cove where there was no bank, only a gentle slope. Out of the water, standing on dry land, I stood quite still, listening for sounds of possible danger. I could only hear the rushing water of the river. There were no lights ahead. I moved inland, keeping an eye on Polaris to know

27

which way I was heading. I was counting my paces to keep track of distance. There was a rice paddy to traverse at first. I thought of eating some but unhusked rice would probably be impossible to digest. I was looking for corn or turnips. Four hundred paces of rice paddy, at most two feet per pace, eight hundred feet through the slime of the paddy before I found corn. I peeled the leaves off an ear that was low on the stalk and thus smaller, less hardened by the sun.

I had eaten two ears before the barking began. Hastily, I looked at Polaris. The dog was between me and the shore. Soon the dog was upon me. He was not very big but he was loud. I talked to him gently, putting out my hand so he could smell it, but he would not be soothed. He went on barking.

'Oh well,' I thought, 'Lord knows when I shall next eat. Might as well have another ear.'

As I ate, I heard the new sound, voices high pitched, excited voices, growing nearer and louder. Then I saw them: little boys, ten to twelve years old, eight of them in all, armed with staves and wearing arm bands. There was silence on both sides when they first saw me. Even the dog stopped barking. I made to stand up and the silence was shattered. The little boys screamed at one another, guttural, shrill military commands. One stooped and took a big rock in his hand. He cocked his arm to throw. The stone flew through the air.

And I was nearly twelve again, just after the degradation ceremony to which my father was subjected. I was following the man who had hit my father then smeared him with excrement. This man and his friends had left the degradation ceremony in high spirits. They stopped at a tavern, asked for water to clean up and loudly reminded one another of their role in the degradation proceedings. Then they ordered food and wine, to celebrate. I crouched in the shadow of a doorway half a block down the street. They had a lot of money and I remember saying to myself that these were their thirty pieces of silver. It was a long celebration continuing on to dusk and it broke up because they obviously could absorb no more. The man who had hit father stood, uncertainly, and made his way for home through ever narrowing lanes ascending to the poorer part of Plaka at the foot of the Acropolis, a part of town I knew well.

Clutching a big rock in my good hand, I followed, taking care that he should not notice—not that he was in a fit state to notice. Finally, he stopped to urinate and I walked up to him. He looked

28

with glazed eyes, not understanding what I was doing stepping into the jet of his urine; and then I hit him hard in the face with the rock. He fell silently on his back, his head thudding hollowly on the ground. What had been his mouth was now red pulp. I picked a handful of horse dung from the street and stuffed it in his mouth, then I made for home. The consciousness of what I had done to a man came late, at night. I rose in my bed feeling in my hand the sensation of the rock crushing his lips, cracking his teeth while his eyes opened slowly in amazement then closed in pain, spouting tears as the neck snapped back, leading the body into a descending arc which ended on the ground with a thud.

The stone thrown by the Korean boy and the stone I had held to hit a man became one. I was the man I had hit. The boys stood in a semi-circle, holding their staves, watching my response to being hit. I had been struck on my chest. I did nothing because there was nothing I could do. A boy of twelve can kill a grown man. Seeing my lack of reaction, the other boys also began throwing stones.

I fell on my knees and extended my hands before me, in supplication. I was terrified. These were not purposeful enemy officials trying to bend my will. These were small boys vying with one another in a game of skill, in which I was the target. So I grovelled, whimpering with fear. Probably the first Gigantes to do so. I should have died. I must have passed out because I remember nothing until I came to, listening to Lavrenti.

At the sound of his voice, I wept with relief. I was being lowered from the back of a truck and Lavrenti was standing there. Sobbing I put out my arms towards him as a child does. He put his arms around me.

Gently, he assured me I was back safe; that I might have been killed by those boys.

With Lavrenti on one side and Kim on the other, I was helped back into the brainwashing room. I was sobbing still, I remember, but I do not remember much else. There is a gap in my memory until they tied me to the chair. As the telephone wire bit into my wrists, I was myself again and Lavrenti was berating me.

I was being unreasonable and ungrateful, he said. I had attempted to escape, nearly got myself killed; had come back exhausted, then the minute they were out of the room, I tried to hang myself. Didn't I realise I was not even fit enough to commit suicide?

I had tried to commit suicide? How? When? Was it true?

'I don't believe you,' I said.

They showed me the loop of electric wire over the transom, with a chair beside it.

'You put those things there, I did not.'

I simply did not remember.

'You mean you don't remember doing it, Mr Deane?' When they came into the room, I was standing on the chair and had the wire in my hands, Lavrenti said.

Where would I get the wire?

I had ripped it off the wall, it seems, and fused half the house.

I did not, I said. I would remember it, if I had tried to kill myself.

'But you did try. All of us here saw you on the chair.'

Were they serious? Had I tried to kill myself? Lavrenti sounded so positive. They had started the brainwashing again with Lavrenti presiding. What were we talking about, anyhow? The sound of his voice came to me then went, then came again like a pendulum of sound. Was it my voice, and what was it saying? My memories of what was happening were scanty even immediately after the brainwashing process came to its end. But these scanty memories remain with me.

I was having thoughts of giving in but I was not sure how much I should give in, or rather, how much they would expect me to give in. After all, they seemed convinced I was a spy and they would probably not be satisfied with a broadcast or broadcasts about what I had seen the American pilots do to Korean villages. But were they convinced I was a spy? Perhaps they were not and they were simply using this technique to increase the pressure of fear. Perhaps I should have seen this doubt of mine about the spy motif as a ray of hope: on the contrary, not knowing whether or not they really believed I was a spy increased my anxiety. It was almost as if I would have preferred them to have believed I was a spy. The uncertainty about their beliefs seemed harder to face than the very serious charge of espionage.

In the early stages I had been able to feel detached and to study what was happening in that room, as if I were a reporter, covering a story. I am not speaking here of the various dissociations when I was two separate minds, but the periods when I was one mind that was being attacked and could see the peripheral aspects of the situation, smell the brilliantine on

Lavrenti's hair and derive some amusement at this habit of his; watch Mr Pak screaming and look at his quivering epiglottis thinking it funny; deliberately make Pak angry and feel a sense of power from this; treat Lavrenti's story-telling with the contempt it deserved.

Exhaustion by now was so complete that I was losing control: I sobbed often, for instance. I sobbed with relief when Lavrenti would say that he felt sorry for me and wanted to help me, that if I would agree to co-operate, he would speak on my behalf to the Korean authorities. I found myself thinking he was a friend, a man who had some cultural affinities with me whereas Kim and Pak had none. And yes, I had the racist feeling that because he and I were both white, he would, ultimately, stand by me against the yellow men.

He continued telling me about Boris and Natasha. I remember only snatches of what he said but I clearly remember that I no longer listened to his story with critical detachment. Quite quickly, I began identifying completely with Boris and felt that Lavrenti was on Boris' side and therefore on mine as the description of Natasha's love affairs continued: she tried various men, a physician, an engineer who smelled, a near half-wit, her grandmother's husband (or was it Boris' father, a picturesque old rogue of a Cossack chief). Finally she found her true love, a man with a withered leg who could not, thus, join the armed forces.

The injustice to Boris was, I felt enormous: that he, a whole man and fine physical specimen could be supplanted in his wife's affections by a cripple seemed monstrous. I remember Lavrenti insisting that cripples have a tremendous sexual drive to compensate for their physical disability—being unable to beat other men physically, they beat them sexually. I remember feeling that this was so unfair to Boris—that this particular cripple would seek to affirm his manhood in my wife's bed. Lavrenti agreed that it was unfair and I remember looking at him with gratitude for this instance of comprehension. I looked forward to the next instalment of the Boris-Natasha melodrama, the instalment that Lavrenti recounted and not Kim's repetitions. Kim would stress certain aspects of what Lavrenti had told me before. Kim made me cry a great deal. I do not know this, but I assume that he was repeating those passages which Lavrenti had marked down as affecting me most. Pak would then scream at me, one phrase or two, the most painful ones. Once, only

31

once, I regained enough control to remember sensing that Pak was clearly embarrassed by having to scream descriptions of the sexual act.

Lavrenti would then come in and ask me to whom I was being loyal. To a wife who was cuckolding me? I seem to remember his saying quite often that they had asked their people to check on my wife and that they had received detailed reports that she was indeed cuckolding me. I was too far gone, by then, to challenge such an assertion on the grounds that it seemed highly unlikely to me that the Soviet government would have its agents check on the private life of a prisoner's spouse. My father, Lavrenti said, would betray me, my mother too and all those I had considered friends. My employers would certainly not remain loyal to me. They would not set aside my salary. I was suffering for the sake of people to whom I meant little or nothing. I believed him, most of the time.

It is strange to think that one can be made to believe such things. It is paradoxical, to say the least, that I could believe my mother would betray me. There was no possibility of such a thing occurring; nor was there a circumstance in which such betrayal could occur. But the stress on me after my attempted escape was greater than before.

I was now continuously tied to a chair. I remember Lavrenti and Kim discussing the reasons why, in my presence. This was one of my more lucid moments and I asked why they talked to one another in English.

He did not know Korean, Lavrenti said, and Mr Kim, though fluent in English and German, knew no Russian. Indeed, I had noticed before they always greeted one another in English when they relieved one another behind the desk whereas Mr Pak and Lavrenti exchanged salutations in Russian.

Lavrenti and Kim discussed, in my presence, the advisability of keeping me tied to a chair. I had tried to commit suicide, after all, Kim said, and tried to escape, Lavrenti added. But they did not worry about my trying either of those things again. They feared I might soil the room again, however, while they were away. They spread a piece of linoleum under my chair to prevent impregnating the wooden floor with excrement. Each time I defecated, the interrogator would leave the room and the guards would make me clean up, as roughly as they had made me clean up the first time I had soiled myself. Only now it was a much more taxing process for me. Walking to the courtyard meant falling nearly every other step. Then, with a full bucket, I would start back towards the house, fall, lose the water, again and again: all this as the guards screamed at me and other guards came round to watch the spectacle.

After each such episode, it would be Lavrenti who would meet me.

'Why make yourself suffer?' he would ask, kindly.

'You do not want to suffer, do you? And I hate seeing you suffering this way.'

He always brought tears to my eyes when he said that.

'And for the sake of what are you suffering? To whom are you being loyal?'

Then he would be off again on the story of Boris and Natasha.

Boris called his children 'the beloved turnkeys' who kept him and Natasha locked in a terrible marriage, said Lavrenti.

In my condition, I found this particular piece of the melodrama deeply affecting and sobbed freely, pitying Boris, pitying myself. Kim took up the theme, stressing details and then Pak would chime in with his screaming. I cannot remember if he was still embarrassed by the sexual details. I do remember that I began having a nightmare, or perhaps I should call it an hallucination since I was not asleep: I was trying to escape and a huge pair of female buttocks would fall on my face, preventing me from breathing. Between the thighs that grew from those buttocks lay a male with a withered leg, fornicating. I remember screaming each time the hallucination came. After my screaming bout, Lavrenti would come in: he must have slept in his clothes since he was always available. He would commiserate and urge me to put an end to my suffering by collaborating.

Would I promise to broadcast and tell the world about the 'barbarous American attacks' I had seen against unarmed Korean villages?

This I could not promise. Time after time I could not make that one specific promise. The reasons were different. More than once, I could not make the promise Lavrenti wanted because of one American I had known, Homer Davis, who had run the school I attended in Greece.

I did not remember Homer Davis as a lovable old schoolmaster. There is a delight in caring for one's former teacher, a kindly and somewhat cruel delight at reversing roles and scoring the passage of the generations. Students, banded together, recount raucous episodes in class, fondly recall a teacher's oddities. Books have been written full of not unadmirable sentiment about the old master who gave his prime passion to nurturing youth. There was none of that in my feelings towards Homer Davis.

I cannot remember ever discussing him as a sweetly funny relic. I do not even see him in retrospect as part of my child world, one of the patient images, conveniently there for us to feed upon, feed on their knowledge and on their emotions which we so carefully tapped, then ignored. The relationship between student and good teachers is much like that between tyrannical child and long-suffering grandmother; it is enjoyed by both and is a great bond.

Homer Davis did not fit this picture. The memories of him were very few: he would walk out of his office and find me pacing the hall in punishment, round and round. He would always stop, grin, and ask 'Again?'

On another occasion we were losing a basket-ball game in which I was playing, and having missed a shot I swore. Dr Davis heard me and said: 'That's bad sportsmanship,' then added frowning, 'but dammit, I hate to see us lose.'

Thinking back on what he gave me, I could remember he had encouraged me to be more stubborn, more competitive, more unreasonable in many ways than I already was; I think he also encouraged in me a certain unconcern for my own welfare or ease. It was not an elaborate process on his part—just an occasional and very curt demand that I do better, and an amused smile when I did too much, as when he let me use English extravagantly in the school paper—it read like Roget's Thesaurus—or allowed me to write on politics, involving myself and the school in some trouble with the authorities. He enjoyed the ridicule of my predicaments.

A stubborn, unreasonable, even competitive fear of losing his good opinion of me kept me from breaking down—that and the sense of ridicule, a very Aristophanian, very Greek sense of ridicule which this man gave me. Even a tormentor could be funny.

Homer Davis was a fully conscious memory, in moments of lucidity. There were the unconscious dissociations too, always of uncle Yanis or father: I was out of the chair, soaring, nearly twelve again, just after father's unsuccessful coup and his death sentence. Fists were pounding our front door. We opened.

'Dress,' the gendarmes said to my mother. 'You do not have much time. They will shoot your husband at dawn.' Mother then vanished from the dissociation and I was with father. He had asked to see me alone for a while and the orderly had decently given up his office for the interview.

'Take your time,' he said. 'You may have as much as two hours. These things are never on time.' He bowed out of the room smiling uncomfortably, a gaunt man with a bony chin and gnarled hands protruding from black oversleeves he wore to keep his cuffs clean as he filled in the register at night. It lay there, the register, a large cloth-bound book, on a plain wood table over which shone a bulb hanging beneath a green glass shade. The floor was made of tiles long cracked and for years no government had spent money to paint this prison orderly room. We sat on a long wooden bench and my father talked.

'Are you afraid, my boy?'

'I must not be?'

'You can be,' he said. 'And you probably are. There is nothing wrong in being afraid. You must not show it, that's all.'

'Are you afraid father?'

He smiled brilliantly. 'Of course I'm afraid, but they won't know it.'

'People have told me you have never been afraid of death.'

'It's not death I am afraid of so much,' he said, 'it's that I am not too sure I am dying for the right reasons.' He saw the bewildered look on my face and added: 'Perhaps I shouldn't be talking like that to you. You are too young to be troubled, at this moment, with my doubts but my doubts are all I know and I may never again have time to tell you about them.'

'But I thought you were fighting for democracy,' I said, and I had trouble with my voice. 'Niko—the maid's boyfriend, you know—says you are like Harmodios and Aristogeiton who killed the tyrant in ancient Athens and died for democracy.'

Lakis Gigantes laughed. 'I should hope not. Poor Niko does not have much schooling and has not read his Thucydides. Harmodios and Aristogeiton did not die for democracy. They killed the wrong tyrant over a homosexual lover's quarrel and later everyone made them into heroes of democracy. I would like to think I am dying for democracy.'

'But is that not what you are dying for, father?'

'Am I? Or was it power? I wish I knew.'

35

Not knowing what to say, I told father what I had done to the man who had slapped him during the degradation ceremony.

'That was vengeance,' father said. 'Vengeance is always a waste of time.'

We were interrupted by the orderly who came, flushed with excitement, to announce that the death sentence had been commuted to life imprisonment.

'Shit,' said father, 'all that rehearsing for nothing. I was going to recite François Villon's *La Ballade des Pendus*. They've spoiled my last scene.'

Later I had made a point of learning the words. Soaring still, I recited them.

I was hallucinating, said Lavrenti to Kim : it will not be long now. The hallucinations come close to the end.

This was my penultimate lucid moment. Between that moment and the last lucid moment I had during brainwashing there was a period of time about which I remember very little except that I had the feeling of re-enacting the legend of my uncle Yanis' death in 1943.

On that cold winter night, there were only the smell of misery in the street and the whisperers. These hugged the walls, seeking the deepest shadow, moving from door to door, briefly scratching, telling the news : their leader had been betrayed and the hounds of hell in the black uniforms with the skull and crossbones were, this moment, after him.

Women who were believers, later said they spilled a little of their precious olive oil into a wick to light before an ikon and pray on their knees that the leader might escape. He too had heard the whispers and rather than vanishing like a ghost as he so often had, he stayed to burn the papers he had that day received with the new codes, the names of stalwart men who were to help, and the dates of major raids.

Not all the paper was calcinated when the whine of trucks filled the air, ringing the whole block, and the dank January night was dispelled by the cold light of arc lamps. The hunters had come in force. The building where the leader was, the adjoining ones, the whole street stood pale and shabby in the glaring light. It was long since paint had touched the stones and the woodwork. Window panes, begrimed, looked in the light like the tired eyes of very old men and occasionally an eye was blind—a broken window pane, impossible to replace, its space plugged opaquely by paper or cloth, unseeing. Through the glass, wherever there was glass, gaunt faces looked on, eerily leprous as the shadows of the dirt on the windows fell on flesh. One enemy hunter who did not like the sight gestured menacingly with his machine pistol at the rows and rows of faces that stared down upon the beleaguered building. It was a futile gesture for no face moved from its window.

Finally, the hunters covered all the roofs, back courtyards, the alleys, and the searchers burst into the apartment building. They knew he was there but they did not know in which apartment. It was a sergeant who knocked on the quarry's door. Yanis Gigantes, leader of the Greek underground, answered the summons and asked in flawless German what the search was about.

'Papers!' the searcher said, tightening his grip on his pistol. Slowly, with just two fingers, Yanis Gigantes moved his jacket sideways exposing the inner pocket and with the other hand took out his official pass as interpreter for the German court martial.

At the sight of the swastika, the searcher relaxed but only momentarily. It was after he rifled through the booklet that he began to smile. He was a very young man, on his first important assignment and he wanted to talk about it. There were ears that heard what he said and recorded it.

'Forgive me for having disturbed you, sir. You will understand that I am only doing my duty. But we have been told that in this building, there hides the leader of the Greek underground, that notorious criminal, and tonight we are going to capture him and destroy his organisation.'

'I wish you the very best of luck,' said Yanis Gigantes, 'the man you are seeking is an evil man and a stupid man who refuses to understand that the order of the Third Reich is Europe's only hope. Heil Hitler.'

A gust of wind, the cold insidious wind of the Athenian January, blew down the chimney into the stove where the leader's documents were being consumed and the smell of burning paper, riding a draught, traversed the apartment all the way to the front door. The young sergeant had been well trained. The smell of burning paper during a search was a suspicious event to be investigated. But he had not been trained well enough.

'What is that?' he said harshly digging at Yanis Gigantes with the barrel of his pistol. And then the young sergeant slipped by, running towards the fireplace. Yanis Gigantes shot him in the head.

It is not true that people die instantly with a bullet in the brain. Life wants to live. Death is not instant. The legs continue their motion, the hands clutch the air, clawing to pull life out of the closing darkness. And the air in the lungs and the abdomen rises up shivering the vocal chords in one last raucous call for life to continue.

Yanis Gigantes, now with only five bullets left in his service 38, walked to the front door of the apartment building. There were shots from enemy searchers who had climbed to higher floors and who aimed at him down the stair well. Tenants watching him through cracks in the doors, swore later that his walk was stately, the ceremonial gait of the military college. They felt he was very conscious of being on stage, of playing his last act. He stood poised for one brief moment before the door that led to the street, pushed it open and walked out, his gun blazing.

Yanis Gigantes was extremely short-sighted. He was also vain and so he was wearing a monocle rather than glasses. It is, thus, a matter of no small wonderment that with each of his five bullets, he hit an opponent in the heart. It was said, afterwards, that he aimed with his Greek soul and had no need for eyes.

It was also a matter of no small wonderment that his opponents were firing at him with machine pistols and that his chest and head were covered with blood, witnesses said, while he was still erect and still firing. The legend which sprouted in his blood would have it that he was dead after he fired his second bullet but that even in death such a man could exact a price from the enemy.

There was a whimper of shots while enemies fired into him as he lay on the ground. And then silence. Doors creaked open and the people came out to stare at the remains of the man whose exploits had made hearts leap. By one of those monumental errors of which the military mind is capable, the enemy commanding officer—another Creon—decreed that Yanis Gigantes should not be buried but should be left to rot in the street. Interpreters shouted the order that this was to be an example of how rebels would be punished. It had all been said, long before, in *Antigone* :

> *touching this man*
> *it has been ordained*
> *that none shall favour him*
> *with sepulcher or tears*

38

but leave him there exposed
garbage that
the dogs shall eat
a ghastly sight of shame.

Nothing happened for a while and no one knows how long that while lasted. Then, singly, in twos and threes and throngs the women of Athens came from side streets, along the main boulevard on which Yanis Gigantes lay. The women had all made an effort to wear mourning. There are professional keeners in Greece but there were none among these women. There were no sobs, no cries just silence and some tears. Most bore a tribute, a sprig of basil, a pine branch, some laurel leaves. Others brought carefully tended pots of flowers that had been nursed through winter by a sunny window. The enemy guard around the body tried to fend off the mourners.

Somehow, the young enemy soldiers seemed unable to use their normal tactics : no blows were struck with butts of weapons; no boots lifted to bruise the flesh. There is, perhaps, a universal revulsion at sacrilege, and, before heroism, an awe that absolutist dogma cannot obliterate.

Like Creon's son, the young guards balked at their appointed task. And so, the Antigones of Athens knelt by the remains of Yanis Gigantes. They had brought candles, a rare commodity in that 1943 January of privation. The street became a carpet of tapers. One voice, then another struck up the Epikedios, the funeral hymn of the Orthodox church.

Then they lifted him and, bearing him shoulder high, walked in the night lighted by their candles, the long distance to the cemetery. The news had spread and, along the route, the flickering flames of devotional oil wicks shone in the windows.

As if they had known in advance, the women made their way unerringly to an unoccupied plot and there buried him, as Antigone had interred her brother :

no cut of shovel tore that earth
no pick dug up and split that ground
the soil was virgin, unbroken, without mark
the dead man covered
not lowered in a tomb
but thinly sprinkled with the dust
as if by someone who avoids a curse.

39

During my hallucinations in the brainwashing room, I was my uncle Yanis, walking out of the apartment building and there were Lavrenti, Kim and Pak, firing at me with machine pistols and I was shooting back, dying but still aware of all around me; and the women of Athens were mourning me, then burying me. And after the vision, there would always be Lavrenti's voice:

. . . Why not be reasonable? You agree that I want to help you. You agree that you want me to help you. Why won't you promise to broadcast? . . . I forgot how many times this happened. It seemed to be happening often, though I do not know over what length of time. Sometimes I would be fully dressed while being my uncle Yanis, sometimes I would be naked and covered with excrement. In either case, I was the central figure in a procession of honour to my tomb.

Eventually I had my last lucid moment. I was one, no longer on the chair, no longer naked. I was, I think, on a bed, but I felt insubstantial. I can only compare the feeling to being drugged heavily with morphia. Nothing seemed precise. There were no distinct ends or beginning to objects. All was a cloud. And I felt very small physically, as if there were very little of me left. From far away I could hear Lavrenti and Kim talking. But their words were blurred. I knew I was at the end of my endurance. I made the firm decision to give in and I knew clearly what I was doing: I was going to broadcast whatever they wanted. And I knew that after that broadcast, there would be other things they would want me to do and I would do them. I felt immense relief, even joy. Then Lavrenti said: 'He is dying. We must stop. We'll try other methods when he regains his strength.'

'Are you sure he is dying?' Kim asked. 'Of course, you are a physician, but maybe we could go on a little longer.'

'No,' said Lavrenti. 'He could take no more and live to be of any use to us. It's very many days since we first brought him here, a long time.'

'Others have taken it for longer periods, I believe,' Kim said. 'There was mention in the books I read.'

'Probably those others were not wounded. Probably they did not have as much pressure put on them. All I know is that if we continue he will die.' There are conversations one does not forget: that was one.

They let me recover; then they took me to the camp where

40

civilian detainees were kept near Pyongyang, the North Korean capital. From there—in anticipation of Macarthur's landing— we were taken north, first in cattle trucks, then on foot, to prevent our being freed. We were joined with American military prisoners many of whom looked already like Belsen inmates, gaunt, ragged, dirty and hopeless.

Those, perhaps, were our worst moments.

We marched for days and days. Those among us who could no longer walk were shot in the head. We marched, arriving at our destination, Chung Kan Djin, the death camp on November 8, 1950, having left behind more than 100 dead, shot because they were sick.

And the young Americans went on dying. There had been 777 when we joined them in September 1950, and more than sixty per cent of them had died by February 1951.

Eventually, conditions improved. We had more food, some clothes, firewood and vaccinations. In December 1951 I was suddenly taken to Pyongyang the North Korean capital.

It's December 28, I reasoned, they probably want to make a New Year propaganda broadcast to prove they treat prisoners well. They are going to take me to Pyongyang for a third degree. They'll try to make me talk on the radio.

Soon after I arrived, I was marched to the office of the man I came to think of as Mr Han. It was a very big office, some thirty feet by twenty with carpet on the floor. A large conference table with sixteen chairs took up much of the space. The rest was filled by a large desk of light polished wood and three, deep, leather armchairs, flanked by ashtrays on stands. In a corner, I noticed a folded camp bed. The desk was piled with files, books, and desk ornaments, among them busts of Marx, Engels, Lenin and Mao. There was no bust of Kim II Sung the North Korean leader, but a coloured poster bearing his likeness hung framed over Mr Han's chair.

Mr Han was nearly lost in this chair. He also seemed nearly lost in his glasses and his clothes. Everything was too large for him : the tortoiseshell frame of his spectacles slipped constantly on his nose; the collar of his shirt touched his neck nowhere; he wore a pullover that sagged at the shoulders. The cuffs were rolled so as not to cover his hands. He had the distant look of a scholar absorbed in happy contemplation of his favourite problem. Mr Han looked very likeable.

He stood up to greet me, waved me to one of the leather

41

armchairs and poured me a glass of milk from a thermos bottle.

'How are you, Mr Deane?' he asked. He had no accent, just a very deliberate way of speaking.

I said I was as well as could be expected considering that I had been unjustly imprisoned, had nearly died in their hands, had been subjected to torture and intolerable pressure.

Every part of Mr Han's face expressed pain: his tall narrow forehead was suddenly furrowed with anxious lines; his chin seemed to grow longer; his cheeks even more sunken; his eyes nearly shut with distaste; even his sparse hair appeared to writhe in embarrassment.

I must not think of him in terms of pressure, said Mr Han. I would soon realise that our meetings would have nothing menacing.

But did he know what happened to me earlier?

He knew I had been interrogated, said Mr Han, and he squirmed visibly: but our meetings would have no connection with what happened earlier. That was a different department . . . His task was to convert me.

'To convert me? to what?'

'To our way of thinking, Mr Deane.' Thereafter, my conversation, as best I can reconstruct it from my notes proceeded as follows:

'And you believe I could be converted to your way of thinking after what was done to me by the Russian?'

'Yes, Mr Deane.'

'Well, let me tell you now: you will never convert me. A system that subjects a man to what I experienced is inimical to everything I stand for.'

'You reason from the particular to the general, Mr Deane. There has been no system in history which did not have bad aspects at some time or another—especially under pressure of war. There has been no system in history which has not used harsh methods in dealing with spies.'

'But I am not a spy.'

'That is a matter on which you have not convinced the authorities.'

'Do you think I am a spy?'

'It is immaterial to me, Mr Deane.'

'You say you want to convert me. Doesn't it matter what sort of person I am?'

'It matters, Mr Deane. You showed great endurance during

your interrogation. You exhibited certain traits that would make you useful to us.'

'As what?'

'That remains to be determined.'

'You mean that if I am a spy, you would make me a double agent.'

'Why not?'

'I would never play such a role.'

'Why not, Mr Deane?'

'Because it involves working for people and betraying them. It's a matter of loyalty.'

'Of course. But if you are truly loyal and committed to a cause, the harm you do to the enemies of that cause is not disloyalty. If you become a willing convert to our cause you will want to embarrass its enemies.'

'I could never become a true convert to your cause.'

'We shall see, Mr Deane. But let us not say *our* cause, let us say *a* cause. If you are truly loyal to *a* cause, then you would want to embarrass and confound its enemies.'

'Not necessarily.'

'How do you mean?'

'I would not do certain things for any cause.'

'Everyone has such reservations, Mr Deane. I have them myself. There are certain things I will not do for my cause. I am not asked to do those things.'

'I could not believe in a cause that asks *others* to do certain things.'

'The means are not justified by the end, in other words, Mr Deane?'

'Right.'

'But surely this is not an absolute statement : it is relative.'

'Is it?'

'Of course it is, Mr Deane. If you were asked to kill an individual German now because he opposes a cause you espouse—say a united Europe—you would refuse. Yet, in World War Two, I am sure you killed Germans for the sake of your cause . . .'

There were days and days of such dialectics, none of it under pressure. The outside world was far away.

One day I had a visitor. He brought me a letter. It was signed by William Randolph Hearst Junior. Before my capture, Mr Hearst's bureau chief in Tokyo had hired my services as a photographer, at the front. The terms included a monthly retainer

43

plus payments for pictures used. This contract may have accounted for my capture: to take action pictures, I had taken greater risks than I would have had to take as a reporter.

Mr Hearst's letter read as follows:

'Deane, you must not assume that you are still on our payroll. Payments to you stopped as of the day you were captured. William Randolph Hearst Jr.'

Now, I can say that Mr Hearst did not have much of an obligation towards me: I was only a casual employee. But I remember that when I received his letter I felt bitterly resentful; not because he was cutting off the money but because he had not even bothered to say 'good luck' or 'best wishes for a quick release' or some such thing. He did not know me at all, admittedly, but I was a prisoner and I had worked for him. He had taken the trouble to send me a message but his message was like a letter from a collection agency. I am not saying that I *should* have expected anything else; but, in fact, when I read the letter, I was struck hard by its dryness and I remembered that when I was brainwashed I was told that no one would be loyal to me while I was a prisoner.[3] This message made me feel closer to Mr Han: maybe that is why the communists had let that message through.

Eventually, we had our last meeting. Mr Han made of it a ceremony. He had two cups on a table, such cups as are used to drink Chinese tea. There was a flagon which contained, he said, apricot flavoured wine. He filled my cup then his and wished me a quick return to my home. I answered his toast in Greek:

'Hoti epithymeite.'

'What does that mean?'

'It means "whatever you desire", Mr Han. It is a Greek toast.'

'Why did you call me "Mr Han"?'

'You have not told me your name. I have come to think of you as Mr Han.'

'Do I remind you of a particular Mr Han?'

'No.'

'Then why do you call me Han?'

'You have talked of Chinese civilisation and have done so most ably, if I may say so. It is the Han civilisation, is it not? I think of you as the Han civilisation.'

It was obvious that Mr Han was torn between feeling flattered and feeling insulted: he was not sure I was being serious. He could not stoop to asking me whether I meant what I said and

44

I had used a tone which, I knew from experience, left him in doubt about my meaning. He struggled visibly with himself and his self esteem won. He tugged at his sleeves, looked modest and finally smiled shyly but with obvious pleasure.

He said it was the last time we should see each other and I said I was sorry which caused him to express surprise. I explained that while we had spent our time disagreeing, I had found him civil and interesting.

This time he knew I was not being ambiguous : I had paid him a sincere compliment. His eyes closed with pleasure. He leaned his head backwards and sucked in air through his teeth in sibilant appreciation. His eyes wrinkled in a smile and he showed me all his teeth.

He answered that he too would be sorry at our parting because though I made our conversations difficult, I had not lacked in intellectual respect, but had listened attentively to him. My expressions of disagreement had been forceful but that was good : that was the way of resolving contradictions.

I said we had not resolved any that I was aware of, and he replied that maybe a seed he had sowed would burgeon in my mind and I would see the truth. Thoughtfully he sipped his wine. He did not think I was a wicked man, he added : my heart would lead me to the truth, his truth.

We sat together in the draught between two open windows. It was on the 9th of July, 1953, and the atmosphere was oppressive even though there was no cloud. Far above, in the blue sky, a thin, lengthening vapour trail marked the path of a high-flying jet.

The US is a monstrous society, Mr Han said, summing up the millions of words he had spoken. America glorified greed. All it cared about was getting richer. It did not have qualms of conscience about the way its negroes, Indians and other underprivileged groups were treated. It demonstrated, in Korea, a total and very racist disregard for human life. America used the atom bomb on Japan, on yellow people. Humanity would be better off if, instead of being ruled by greed, it were ruled by a sense of duty on the part of each human being towards other human beings.

There was a knock on the door and food was brought in. I had not seen such a meal in two years. It was a Chinese meal and there were five different courses as well as a large bowl full of white rice. Mr Han arranged the dishes on the table and

45

picked out delicacies with his chop sticks to put before me. He appeared to be searching for some system: from which bowl to serve me first? But this task was like the other small unimportant aspects of life—he could not manage it and it vexed him. He dropped a piece of beef into the fish, splattered his finger, picked up a piece of paper to use as a serviette and, after using it, discovered it was a document he needed. He searched his pockets for some of the paper handkerchiefs he carried and some small keys fell on the floor. At that point he gave up, smiled sheepishly and gestured that I should help myself. We ate silently, while he recovered his composure and then he asked what was my interpretation of history, after all those hours of talk together.

I said that man, to be an individual, needed freedom. But most men were also members of a society which needed order. The conflict between freedom and order is the human dilemma. I did not want the individual to win and I did not want society to win. I wanted them to remain in a state of tension, in conflict.

I saw it was my duty to take part in the conflict, to defend the side which was losing. Currently, with society becoming more and more complex and various authorities becoming even stronger, I thought it my duty to intervene in the conflict on the side of the individual because each man's individuality was being threatened. I said I thought that, in the West, I and other individuals stood a better chance to oppose authority successfully and thereby defend individuality.

That was an illusion I had, said Mr Han. The individual in western society has no real power with which to oppose authority, especially the individual citizen of the small country. I would see when I put my theory to the test.

INTERLUDE

The test that Mr Han spoke about in 1952 came twelve years later, the test of whether the individual can expect more respect for his rights, and small nations can expect to be freer in the western world under American leadership rather than in the communist world—the test of freedom, as I came to think of it. During those years I first roamed the hemispheres as a newspaper correspondent, leading a life that seemed marvellously rich to my fellow Greeks who were reading my syndicated *Observer* despatches from Afghanistan, Siam, the USA, Burma, North Africa, despatches on Khrushchev's antics, Dulles' power politics, Kennedy's rise, about great men like Nehru, spectacular shooting stars like Che Guevara and corrupt dictators like Trujillo of the Dominican Republic and Batista of Cuba.

It was the sort of journalistic career I had dreamed about, but it was not just a job because the public life I reported on had replaced, for me, most aspects of what constitutes a private life : my marriage had gone the way my brainwashers had said the marriages of prisoners go, despite the two children of the marriage who became 'the beloved turnkeys' who kept my wife and me locked in that marriage.

Because the job and its content were so important to me, it became an intolerable job : one cannot 'live' one's stories quite so much. Perhaps I was deluding myself, but I was assuming a good deal of moral responsibility for what I saw wrong around me. I tried to right wrongs, through journalism, and when I saw that I or the job did not have the power to right wrongs, I tired of the job. I admit now that such an attitude was naive, perhaps arrogant.

At the 1964 Republican presidential convention in the US, the delegates screamed their hatred at the television cameras, called the journalists arrogant. During Mr Nixon's battles with the press, segments of the public wrote to the newspapers, accus-

47

ing them of arrogance. Come to think of it, a journalist's job can easily be perceived as arrogant: he always casts the first stone; the stylistic conventions of his trade demand that he appear impersonal and detached from what he reports—detachment is often confused with arrogance by those from whom one stands detached and, in the case of journalists, this may be a correct perception because we journalists get drawn by the dynamics of our profession into seeing ourselves as being apart from the world around us. It is, inevitably, an irritating attitude but it is also a powerful habit most of us find impossible to break, even when we know we are in its grip: we simply do not know how to write in any other way; we do not know how to *be* in any other way, how to stop *being* outsiders, uninvolved.

Some of us—I for one—find this condition of uninvolvement extremely lonely and we leave journalism (for ever to regret this leaving), seeking involvement only to find that our journalistic traits have made us outsiders for good. At any rate, I left journalism in 1961 to seek involvement as an employee of the United Nations, when the world organisation still seemed to be playing an important role, trying to prevent great power intervention in the Congo.

PART TWO

GREECE

Each conversation in the section which follows is based on extensive notes I made as soon after the conversation occurred. I knew, almost from the first that I would write a book about the experiences I am about to describe and made it my business to maintain a record. To protect innocent people, I kept the existence of this record secret for many years, while the junta ruled Greece.

I was in Washington, director of the UN information centre, when, one spring day in 1964, my life plans were changed by the telephone: the test Mr Han had predicted was on, though I did not know it yet.

The phone call had been startling:

'The King needs you.' The speaker was a high official who still does not want his name revealed.

'Which King?' I asked.

'King Constantine of Greece, naturally.'

'What does he want of me?'

'His Majesty will want to tell you himself, Mr Deane. He would like you to fly to Greece as soon as possible.'

'Can you tell me, roughly, what this is all about?'

The official said he could not speak for His Majesty but possibly I was wanted to work within the frame of the reforms of the monarchy that the King contemplated. He had just ascended the throne after the death of his father and was allegedly anxious to implement some reforms. I lost nothing by flying to Greece and talking with His Majesty, the official said. The King was most anxious to see me, having read and admired much of what I had written.

Writers are particularly vulnerable to flattery, especially journalists who see themselves as quasi-consecrated objective critics of politics. I flew to Greece. And I began taking the careful and extensive notes on which the following pages are based.

My father was waiting at the airport. 'What is this I hear about your going to work for the King? He comes from a family of vipers.'

'He's only twenty-four years old, father.'

'All right—he is a young viper.'

'I haven't accepted a position in the palace yet, father. I have come, simply to talk with the King, that's all.'

51

'Don't accept anything. Ask for time to think before you give an answer.'

I promised and took a taxi to the office of the King's private secretary, Major Michael Arnaoutis, an officer of legendary heroism in the Korean war. I was early and we talked, naturally, of Korea.

'They brainwashed you,' the major said. 'The CIA says you did not break. We're proud of you. Tell me, what is it like? Do they use physical torture?'

Not in the strict sense of the word. The theory—and I learned the theory after I came out of prison—is that they can act on the mind of the prisoner by exploiting fears he already has or implanting other fears. They confront the prisoner with these fears night and day, till he breaks . . .

A buzzer sounded: the King was ready to see me.

The office of King Constantine, on the ground floor of the palace, was a huge room with a high ceiling, a large desk, six telephones, a thick rug—a cross between a library in a London men's club and a Victorian salon.

His Majesty stepped forward and ground my hand in his— I was to learn later that he was a devotee of karate. He seemed at his ease, a tall, healthy, handsome, good-humoured young man with fine manners, a knack for listening as if he enjoyed what he heard, and a gift for easy familiarity. He offered me a long, thin, twisted cigar, coffee, asked about my trip over, my job at the UN, my family. His toy poodle came in and we discussed the possibility of mating his dog with my poodle bitch: I was not attracted to the prospect because the King's dog was not as well bred as mine. Finally he offered me a job. He said he wanted me to act as a contact between himself and the trade unions, the intelligentsia, the press; to open up channels which would enable the King to hear the viewpoints of important segments of his people.

'You will want some time to think the matter over,' said the King. 'Come and see me tomorrow afternoon and give me your answer.' I had wanted to ask for time to think but I did not have to: the King was too well mannered not to sense what would be easiest for me.

By pre-arrangement, father was waiting for me at Floca's, his favourite café.

'We'll take a ride in a car,' he said. He hailed a taxi and told the driver to take us to the north coast of Attica.

'I want to show you a beautiful location,' father said, 'not spoiled by tourists.'

'I know the place, father.'

'You have not seen it since there has been reforesting.' For the next hour he talked resolutely about reforestation, parks, the need to improve Athens by obliging all owners of empty lots to hide them behind fences covered with ivy, morning glory and honeysuckle. I tried to introduce other subjects but he would brook no digressions. Nature, he kept on repeating, was beautiful and since I had been away from Greece, he wanted to share my joy in seeing beautiful spots.

We stopped finally. Under a stiff breeze, the sea was skittish, flecked with foam, a cobalt blue against the azure sky. Islands, modelled by the sun, stood out gnarled and ochre, splashed here and there with white villages.

We made for the beach at father's suggestion. He showed me the back of his cigarette package on which he had written: 'Did anyone plant a microphone on you? Don't say anything. Just check for blobs of chewing gum on your shoes and for other things that should not be on your person.'

I wanted to protest but he looked so obviously earnest that I complied.

Father was pleased that there were no microphones on me. He added that the sound of waves would completely baffle long range listening devices.

I asked who would be trying to listen in on us.

'The King's people: whatever the King has said to them about his reasons for wanting to hire you, they will worry—you are, after all, the son of a man who toppled kings. Then the Queen Mother might want to know what we are saying. Then there is Papadopoulos.'

'Papadopoulos who?'

'He is a colonel. He has served in the Greek Central Intelligence Agency. The Americans have given him a lot of money with which to buy the Greek Intelligence Agency. He has used it to give himself a personal network.'

'Why?'

'Why? Papadopoulos' nickname among his fellow officers is "Nasser", son, and he likes the nickname.'

'Again, what possible interest could Papadopoulos have in me?'

'If you are going to work for the King, Papadopoulos will be

53

interested in you. He is interested in everyone who might wield power or influence.'

'I shall certainly not be wielding power, even if I accept a job at the palace, father. And I doubt I shall have much influence. It takes years to become influential.'

'You might also find out things that Papadopoulos would not like you to know.'

'Like what?'

'Like who works for Papadopoulos in the palace, son. The King's valet, for instance, has an official salary of sixty dollars a month and he drives a new Mercedes Benz. Who gives the valet that kind of money?'

'Maybe the King gave his valet a present.'

'Maybe, but I doubt it. It's too big a present. Then there are the retainers, the CIA pays various personages in the palace.'

'Come on, father! Why should they need a retainer from the CIA? And if they are receiving it, wouldn't they make sure that no one would know? How would you know?'

'I have my own network, too; not as good as Papadopoulos', in the sense that I don't know everything; but occasionally I receive some good information. Many officers who served under me occupy posts in which they see small portions of the truth. I make them talk then I put together the pieces of the truth I get from each, like a jigsaw puzzle. Even some of Papadopoulos' friends are former subordinates of mine. They idolize me,' father concluded, with satisfaction.

'How do you know that your information is good?'

'Because certain sources of information have turned out to be true so often that I believe them, son. Don't forget that I was chief of intelligence at the general staff myself. I know a good source from a bad one.'

'Even good sources of information turn out to be wrong, father, as you know. Besides, I can't believe that personages in the palace would take such a risk.'

'Why not?'

'Well, suppose it became public that they were receiving money from a foreign government, wouldn't that be damaging to the palace? After all, it would practically be treason.'

'No one could make the charge stick. They would deny it, indignantly, and so would the Americans. The accusers would risk jail.'

'I have met these personages more than once. I don't believe

54

that of them, father. Besides, you have met them quite frequently. You seem to like them. How can you think they would be in the pay of a foreign government?'

'I liked them, all right. But don't forget that this palace has worked for foreign governments before,' and he listed their misdeeds. The Greek Royal Family supported the Kaiser in the first war when it was against the interest of Greece to do so. There were documents of the German ministry of foreign affairs which showed that the Greek Royal Family received forty million gold marks to support the Kaiser. That money never found its way into the Greek exchequer—it went into the private accounts of the Family. The Greek Royal Family even agreed to let the Bulgarians take territory from Greece, which was high treason.

'I don't like to think of you in the palace,' father said.

'Why don't you try to think of what good could possibly come out of my taking a job in the palace?'

He conceded that some good might come of it if I decided to be absolutely cold-blooded and thought of myself first. If I played my cards right, and if I got out at the right moment, then the palace job might give me head start in politics.

So there we were again. How often had father tried to make me a politician? Even when he was in exile, in my teens, and could not talk to me personally on the subject, he had got his brother, my uncle Yanis, to coach me.

Once in 1938 uncle Yanis had put down, in perfect and minute copper-plate, the steps through which I would reach the political pinnacle of the country. At the time, I was fourteen. The list ran something like this:

Always be first at school. A reputation for constant scholastic success is an asset in Greece. Our great liberal prime minister, Venizelos was always first. Our cursed dictator, Metaxas, was always first. Greeks take schooling seriously and they admire those who are top students. In any case, being first is a good habit. See Appendix A. (The appendix contained detailed instructions on studying, note-taking and scoring high marks in examinations: e.g. study the speaking style of each teacher. Use his favourite phrases or constructions in answering his examination questions. He will admire your style, because he admires his own: teachers are human. You will, thus, get extra percentage points.)

You will study law. Greeks are impressed by law and it's a

55

good discipline. You will not necessarily practice law. The diplomatic service might be a better career. You will write about the countries you visit and your books and articles will enhance your reputation.

You will stand for election in your thirties, win and you will be given a junior ministry. See Appendix B. (This appendix had various parts: how to win elections; how to keep being re-elected; how to act as junior minister; how to sniff out possible coups against your government. Though I do not remember my uncle's text in detail, there is not much that I have read about politics which was not neatly summarised by Yanis Gigantes' instructions to me.)

Appendix 'C' I remember vividly because it was my introduction to sex. Uncle Yanis attached sufficient importance to this topic to take time to tell me about it, so as to be sure I understood everything well.

'You are interested in sex by now. Probably you have been interested in sex for some time.'

At fourteen I found it difficult to make conversation with him on the all-important matter of sex. Uncle Yanis, however, did not want an interlocutor, he wanted an audience.

'You must never masturbate,' he said. 'Masturbation is terrible. I masturbated once and I did not do well at all in the exam I had the next day.'

'You failed?' I asked, stricken with awe.

'Don't be stupid,' he answered angrily. 'I have never failed an exam. I got 90% in a mathematics paper. That was the only time I did not get 100%. And that same afternoon we played another school at soccer and because I had masturbated the night before, we lost.'

I did not dwell long on the possibility of his team losing even if he had not masturbated the night before. Uncle Yanis' teams never lost.

'You are a boarder in a boys' school,' he continued. 'There is a good deal of homosexuality in such schools. You must not masturbate and it is even more important that you do not become a homosexual. There are two kinds of homosexuals: those who play the role of the man and mount other men—that's very bad but it is not anywhere near as bad as playing the role of the girl and being mounted. One boy I knew . . .'

Uncle Yanis and father had a fund of parables, cautionary tales about the awful things that happened to anyone who did

56

not follow their code. That boy uncle Yanis knew, had become a homosexual playing the role of a woman and he suffered a fate worse than death: 'He became a monk,' said uncle Yanis, 'a monk in a monastery. Pity. He could have been a great man and a great athlete. But . . .'

We walked in a silence for a while, past two or three sidewalk cafés. Uncle Yanis ogled the ladies at the tables and they ogled him right back. He told me that these women were not a bad bunch, considering the hour; it was his firm opinion that the most beautiful women did not frequent cafés much before eight p.m.

'So,' uncle Yanis resumed, 'since you must not masturbate and must not indulge in homosexuality, you must satisfy your sexual drive by going to the whores. On this piece of paper I have the address of a brothel. The doctor inspects the whores every Saturday morning. If you go there at about noon, your chances of avoiding infection are good. You will, of course, wear a prophylactic. Oh, and don't kiss the whores on the mouth: you never know where their mouth has been. Your father's lawyer will give you the necessary money once a month.'

My sexual drive must have been fairly strong because I visited the brothel the moment the lawyer paid me. I had taken along a friend from school who had received a similar lecture from his father. We approached the brothel with what, we hoped desperately, was a nonchalant air. My friend had decided to smoke a pipe—in the pursuit of nonchalance. It was his first pipe and as we entered the brothel, he was turning quite green.

It was an old house with a curving stairway and worn marble floors. The drawing-room was covered with cerise wallpaper that was moulting. Over the fireplace hung a large painting representing an ample female with one of her breasts bare; she was contemplating a skull. This, I knew at once, was 'Genovefa', the favourite painting of Athenian butchers: the butcher shop without a Genovefa on its walls was rare.

We had been in the drawing-room for a good sixty seconds and I was still trying to look everywhere but at the ladies. I could not now say whether they had been pretty: I was not sufficiently selective. The inescapable fact was that THEY WERE THERE, there with flimsy negligées, no underwear and worn slippers. They were polishing their nails, or playing cards and some wore paper curlers.

'Dammit,' said one of the ladies, the tallest of the group, 'I

57

hoped we would have a quiet hour before the afternoon rush but no, we are invaded by schoolboys on an educational outing.'

'Educational outings are no trouble really,' remarked another of the ladies, a short, plump one. 'Boys that age are like sparrows. It's three minutes of work, no more. Easy money.'

'But look at that one with the pipe,' said the tall one. 'He might be sick in bed. And look at the other one: he can't take his eyes off Genovefa.'

'Take him then. You look like Genovefa. He'll like you. It might only last two minutes. I'll take the other one and see if I can get him out before he's sick.'

The predictions had been accurate. It only took three minutes which became a whole hour in the descriptions we gave our schoolmates.

Sending me to the whores, of course, was all in the cause of politics. 'You go to whores,' uncle Yanis had said, 'so as not to be tempted to fool around with girls of your social circle. Accidents might happen and if you get a girl of good family pregnant when you are older, you might be forced to marry her. Consider the trouble you would be in if she was not rich.'

'What trouble, uncle Yanis?'

'She would not be rich enough to support your political career. Politics cost money. You won't want to borrow that money. You must not waste your energies making it. So you must marry a rich girl who will, preferably, have good political connections. Meanwhile, you go to whores. Married women might be all right, too. If I find one willing to take your sexual development in hand, I'll let you know.'

I had not married money and I pointed out this fact to my father while walking with him on that beach, in the Spring of 1964, discussing the advisability of working for the King of Greece, twenty-six years after my uncle had begun planning my sexual and political development.

'Money is important in politics,' father said, 'but if you are very useful to the party, they'll find a way to finance your election.'

Our excursion to the beach ended inconclusively: I maintained that I could not accept any job with a secret agenda in my pocket; father insisted that if I did not, I would rue the day.

Back at my hotel, I found a summons to the Queen Mother's presence.

58

She received me at the Tatoi summer palace, in the foothills of Mount Parnes, northwest of Athens. I was shown into one of the living-rooms, full of comfortable armchairs covered in prints. There were family photographs everywhere, royal personages posing majestically in operetta costumes; all the pictures had inscriptions: from Bootsy to Tootsy etc.

Her Majesty, Queen Frederika the Queen Mother, came in and I was struck once more by her extraordinary magnetism. From the first time I saw Queen Frederika, when she was still a princess and my school went to sing carols to her and her husband, I had always felt the force that radiates from her person.

She is rather small, with curly hair cut close to her head, a flawless complexion and large blue eyes that have bowled over most people who have met her—most men at any rate.

She was glad I had come, she said. Her son was a good man and would be a good king. He deserved that good people work for him. I would work for him, would I not?

I said I did not know yet.

'Why not?'

I had not thought the matter through.

But what was there to think through?

I wanted to reflect on whether the job would be intellectually satisfying.

How did I define an intellectually satisfying job?

A job that used my brain; a job in which I contributed to the thinking that went into a decision rather than a job in which I merely executed decisions taken by others.

The sort of service I wanted to perform presumed a close relationship with the King, the Queen said. It might take time to build such a relationship. The King did not know what I could do.

On the other hand, I replied, if he did not give me a chance, from the first, to put my judgment at his service, he would not know whether I had good judgment and the right relationship would not develop.

It was a long conversation on trust given or earned, mutual or unilateral. It was an inconclusive conversation which irritated the Queen.

I needed time to think. Up to that point I had not been doing much thinking of my own. My friends in Washington and in the United Nations, whom I consulted, had all urged me to work for King Constantine. Some of the people I consulted seemed to think it would be nice, for them, to have a friend at the palace through whom they might obtain invitations to court functions.

In any event, I agreed to work for the King without having first reached a satisfactory definition of my job which bore the title of Secretary General to His Majesty King Constantine of the Hellenes. It sounded grand, especially to Greeks who know that the title Secretary General is borne in each ministry by the senior-most civil servant. I took the job for a mixture of reasons: curiosity, political ambition; I also felt flattered. 'How many men get asked to serve their King?' my friends all said, 'you cannot turn this down, Philip. You would regret it the rest of your life.' And I was tired of doing as the Romans do, in so many different Romes: in Paris, London, Washington; tired of feeling surprised and—worse—pleased when Frenchmen, Britons or Americans did not treat me as a foreigner. I wanted to come home.

Of course, when I began working for the King, I was not immediately aware that I had begun the test of Mr Han's contention that freedom flourishes no more under America than under Russia. And my initial period in the palace seemed far from such major considerations. Some consequences of my entering the employ of the King were unanticipated.

'I think,' I said diffidently to a palace functionary, 'that I shall miss my plane. I am running late.'

'What flight are you on, Mr General?' (A secretary general in Greece or a director general is always called Mr General.)

'The TWA flight to the US.'

The palace functionary picked up the telephone and ordered the flight control tower to hold the TWA jet until I arrived at the airport. I kept my eyes lowered when, later, I walked to my seat in the big jet.

Then, there was the visit by one of the richest men in Greece. He threw his arms wide open and engulfed me in a tight embrace.

'My dear young friend,' he said, 'how happy I am for the King and for the country that you are His Majesty's Secretary General. I hear you are looking for a house.'

'Yes, I am. They're awfully difficult to find. Do you know of one?'

'Yes I do. That is why I came. It isn't much. It's a little lodge at the end of my park. It's really not good enough, considering the entertaining you will have to do but it might tide you over until you find something more suitable. If you'd like to see it, I shall leave instructions with your chauffeur.'

'How much is the rent?'

'I have never rented it. Why don't you just take it for a while till you find another place and let's forget about the rent.'

'I'm afraid we can't forget about the rent,' I said.

'Why not?'

'Well, you know what Caesar said about his wife . . .'

'Ah yes. Not only honest, but obviously so. Yes, yes. How admirable. The Gigantes have such a scrupulous attitude. It makes me even happier to know you will be occupying such a powerful position. Let us say I charge you three thousand drachmas.'

'Three thousand drachmas!'

My rich new friend sounded alarmed: 'If you think it is too expensive, we'll reduce the price.'

'Not too expensive—unbelievably cheap. I didn't know there were houses to rent for three thousand drachmas—one hundred dollars a month.'

'You might think it is too expensive when you see the house. It isn't much.'

I saw the house later that day. It was detached, furnished, had six bedrooms, six bathrooms, servants' quarters, about two acres of garden ringed by a tall stone wall, and the servants went with the house. I called my 'friend' to say I could not accept.

'But why not?'

'The house is too magnificent. People will talk.'

'But why?' he asked indignantly.

'They will wonder how I can afford such a residence. They might even wonder whether you let me have it as a bribe.'

'But I know I cannot bribe you. And you know I cannot bribe you.'

'You know and I know, but I don't want to stretch the credulity of the rest of Greece.'

I had similar offers of splendid houses from others among my rich, new friends and I had similar conversations with each.

But not all wanted to give. When I tried to exercise a particular right open to all citizens, I discovered that I could not do so unless I paid the public servant in charge.

I decided to see this man who apparently took bribes democratically : the same bribe from everybody. He became quite civil when I told him my name. But he would not give me my rights without a bribe. He was looking at me anxiously. Was I going to blow up, his eyes asked? Was I going to ruin him? I did not. Not that I approved of his taking bribes but I rather admired his courage in trying to shake me down. Later, I found that the bribe-taker had become a fan of mine, lauding my sense of justice and equity. Eventually, he was to render me a service which put him in grave personal danger. But more of that later.

Telephones gave me great trouble. I had five sets on my desk and I wanted one only, connected to my secretary's telephone which would have two exterior lines and one connected to the palace switchboard. The man in charge of such technical matters at the palace was quite shocked.

'But Mr General, a man of your rank cannot simply have one telephone set on his desk. People of your rank have five. The King has six.'

'I only need one.'

'But why?'

'I have only one mouth.'

'What if you are talking on your one telephone and the King wants to talk to you?'

'We can have a special line from the King with a luminous signal. When he calls, I'll interrupt whatever other telephone conversation I have at that time.'

'But Mr General, what if the Grand Chamberlain wants to talk to you while you are talking to the King? The Grand Chamberlain will get a busy signal.'

'I couldn't talk to His Majesty and to the Grand Chamberlain at the same time, could I?'

I got my one phone. My father was furious: 'Do you mean to say that when I want to talk to you, my own son, I have to go through your secretary?'

'Does that upset you, father?'

'Of course it upsets me. No secretary has to give me permission before I can speak to my son.'

'It's not a case of her giving you permission, father; she will connect you immediately if I am not speaking to someone else.'

'You mean you'll make me wait, me Lakis Gigantes, so that you can speak to someone else?'

'You would expect me to, would you not, if I was talking to His Majesty on the phone?'

'The King, yes. You work for him.'

'And the Queen Mother? Would you wait while I spoke to her?'

'All right. The Queen Mother too and the Princesses but no one else.'

'Not even the Prime Minister, father?'

'Especially not him.'

I gave careful instructions to my secretary. She had been warmly recommended to me by the Grand Chamberlain who had even hired her for me before my arrival:

'She is a fine lady, of a very good family, even though her father served in the gendarmerie.' The Grand Chamberlain, like other army officers, looked down on the gendarmes. 'She is the soul of discretion and fidelity and has a nice disposition. She never sulks.'

She was, indeed, a splendid lady, not at all soured by a life everyone assumed to have been difficult. She was discreet. She succeeded in soothing my father's ire whenever he could not get through to me on the phone. She could not type, so I did my own typing. The King, as a result, got very messy copy from me but he never complained: His Majesty knew we had a price to pay for looking after a fine lady of many qualities.

One of these qualities was that she knew, and was known by, many of my older visitors, mostly retired generals, admirals and judges.

The head porter would ring and say that General X wanted to see me. General X had long since retired but he was a national hero, and a fine gentleman. I rushed to the front door and escorted him respectfully to my office. I did not want General X to think that I, personally, or as Secretary General, would be standoffish and anything less than delighted at his visit.

'You look so much like your father, my boy—you will excuse me if I do not call you "Mr General" but I dandled you on my knee when you were a baby. You peed on me regularly.'

I offered him coffee and he accepted several cups. He stayed three hours, till one o'clock when he left for his lunch and siesta. I stayed late at the office to catch up with the work I had not done during the morning. I had, instead, received some very sound advice from my visitor about how to act if ever I was minister of war or public order. I listened, rapt—he was an excellent raconteur. He said I had been very civil and I had to urge him to come again. He did, bringing along another distinguished person out of Greece's not so recent history—this was a judge. I was briefed on justice, military justice, the constitutional aspects of martial law and its applications. They both thought me civil and recommended me to their friends so that I had a stream of distinguished personages, contemporaries, all, of my grandfather. They were men I much admired and whom I could not possibly have turned away. They had served their country well. The least I could do was to make them welcome—even though they kept me from working during normal working hours.

Then I realised how I could both receive them and do my work. I received them in groups: they were quite content to sit in my office, talking of public affairs among themselves. My secretary was particularly effective with them. She showed them unbounded respect and enjoyed their flirting with her: after all, they had flirted with her before the Second World War. The traffic of valets bringing coffee cups was heavy and a hum of relaxed talk wafted from my quarters to other parts of the building. Every now and then, my visitors would interrupt their conversation to ask if I agreed. I would lift my head from the document I was working on, to look at all those shrewd, benevolent eyes staring at me expectantly; I would, of course, always agree. Smiles then would break out in the room and all my visitors would say, aloud, how surprisingly perceptive I had grown.

One day as I sat in my office wondering if I would ever get used to the scarlet velvet and tortured brass motif of its furnishings, I heard a voice raised in anger. Mr Constantine Hoidas, chief of the King's political bureau, burst through the door. I had not met him before: he had been on vacation.

'You will take your secretary out of my offices, do you hear!' Hoidas shouted. 'How can I preserve confidentiality with your secretary sharing a room with mine? How can I keep any secrets when your girl can pry into the King's business for you?'

Mr Hoidas was a tall man. His face, when he was not angry, wore a pensive, romantic and valetudinarian look, much like a starving poet's. He was always impeccably dressed and was prized by hostesses. Not many of them must have seen his face contorted in anger. I asked him whether he wouldn't care to leave my office, cool off, and then return to confer with me.

He went on shouting. The great hall which separated his office from mine began to fill with liveried servants, members of the guard, and other officials of the palace.

'Will you leave,' I asked quietly, 'or do I kick your teeth in?'

He left precipitately, not in fear but to regain his office where he dictated a curt note ordering me to remove my secretary from the office she shared with his.

I typed and sent a letter of immediate resignation to the King. I then cleaned out my desk and went to lunch at one of my favourite taverns where they always had splendid artichoke hearts à la vinaigrette and spring lamb fricassé. I had finished my artichokes and was about to attack my lamb fricassé when a uniformed gendarme arrived.

I recognised him as one of the palace drivers. He came to rigid and noisy attention, delivered a muscular salute, and said quite loudly : 'Her Majesty the Queen Mother wants to see you immediately, Mr General.'

The whole tavern heard. Heads turned. People asked what could be happening that the Queen Mother would have someone fetched from a tavern at the lunch hour. The owner of the tavern rushed forward to assure me that he would have some fresh lamb fricassé for me when I returned and that he would place my carafon of white resinated wine in the refrigerator.

The palace driver put his foot to the floor and we had a hair-raising drive through the streets and out of Athens to the Summer Palace.

What was this resignation business, Queen Frederika wanted to know.

I said that Mr Hoidas had shouted, in front of witnesses, that he could not preserve the confidentiality of his files because my secretary would pry into the King's business on my behalf.

And did I think that was sufficient cause for resigning?

'Yes, Your Majesty.'

'Don't be so touchy.'

I said that Mr Hoidas' statements made my work impossible : each of the persons with whom the King wanted me to establish contacts would have heard of the episode and would be reluctant to deal with a man who could be so openly insulted.

Was there no way we would patch this up, the Queen asked.

There was. Mr Hoidas should apologise to me as publicly as he insulted me.

There was something I should know about Hoidas, said the

Queen. His kidneys did not function well and every so often he had to go abroad to have his blood cleaned by a machine. This was bound to affect a man's temper. So, if he was asked to apologise, he would take it badly—it might affect his health.

'Your Majesty is very considerate and is right to think of Mr Hoidas' health. He shouldn't be made to apologise to me if that would affect his health.'

'Then you are withdrawing your resignation?'

'No, Your Majesty.'

'But I thought you agreed that it might harm his health if he was made to apologise.'

'Of course. The choice seems to be between making him apologise and affecting his health or not making him apologise and ruining my credibility. For humanitarian reasons, I think you should choose not to ruin his health and to let me go.'

'You and Hoidas are acting like children.'

'Then you should let both of us go Your Majesty. You can't have children in the positions Mr Hoidas and I occupy.'

'You are impossible. Your resignation will not be accepted. Get back to your post.'

'I have already cleaned out my desk, Your Majesty. I shall not return to my office unless Mr Hoidas apologises.'

'I don't want to talk to you anymore.'

I bowed backward out of the Queen's presence. She was plainly angry: her cheeks were flushed, her eyes blazing. As in all her other moods, in anger she was striking. I remembered her in the years of strife during the Communist guerrilla war when she worked hard in the hospitals, walked the streets to be with the crowds, visited the Communist prisoners and sat with them during a meal—a meal unusually good because she was visiting—her curly head bent, arguing fiercely: and the angry young men—her masters in dialectics—yielded to her charm and did not make their final telling points. They let her leave in a flush of victory because they could not resist her, even though they considered her the most vital symbol of what they opposed. I climbed in the car waiting for me in the garden of the palace and told the driver not to hurry. There were poppies in the fields and the hills around Athens called the Tourkovounia were green for spring—at least where they still showed as hills and not as tapes of asphalt supporting pustules of cement apartments. I looked for parts I knew when I was small but they were gone. How could my country go, I said aloud, and the chauffeur

66

looked at me anxiously in the mirror: 'I did not catch what you said, Mr General.'

'I was only talking to myself. Make a detour. Pass by a village.'

'Which village, Mr General?'

'Any village that is still a village, with old houses, an old café and a store. And no foreigners.'

'I don't know if there will be no foreigners, Mr General, but I'll try.'

We found a village with old houses and a store that served also as the tavern and café of the place. I stopped and asked for a submarine. The submarine is a thick, sticky white paste made mostly of sugar and some vanilla. It is served in a spoon, dipped in water—that is why it is called submarine. It had been my favourite treat in all the village cafés I had visited as a child. But in 1964 I was forty and the submarine did not taste as good as I remembered. Could it have been so cloying and had I really liked it? Was Thomas Wolfe right? Could one never go home again?

I paid and got back in the car.

'Take me to the restaurant where you found me, please.'

I was interrupted once more, halfway through my lamb fricassé, by another palace driver who took me to see the King. The conversation with the King was much like the conversation with his mother.

The next day I received a message that Mr Hoidas would apologise to me. News of his apology were disseminated to all those who had witnessed the scene between us.

The story swept through Athens—at least through that small part of Athens which cared about court gossip. A gentle lady asked me if I had liked hurting him. I looked at her and was startled by her eyes. They were not resentful nor reproachful. They were inviting. I had seen Hoidas that morning. He had passed by me, tall and straight, very pale, but obviously unbowed. I looked into the lady's inviting eyes again. Was this what had gone between Hoidas and me—the rites of spring, the animal duel? I was sorry I had made him apologise. The lady's invitation stayed unanswered.

'Fool,' my father had said. 'I don't know if Hoidas sleeps with her, but she sleeps with lots of others. She could have helped you. She knows things. You might have learned things that would help you diminish Hoidas.'

'I am not particularly anxious to diminish Hoidas,' I said.

'He's a bloody Corinthian. They cannot be diminished enough.' I had forgotten that my father's political allegiances were Thucydidian—Corinth had been for the Spartans and against Athens in the fifth century BC. For father, Corinthians would be forever suspect. I had once asked him how he could defend such prejudices—he mistrusted Spartans, Thebans and, of course, Corinthians. After all, I had said, there have been many invasions of Greece. Even the blood has changed. People have changed. Nonsense, he had answered: the land was stronger than blood. Corinthians would always be Corinthians—sinister.

They did not look sinister my fellow courtiers—even the Corinthians among them. They were, on the whole, pleasant to work with in the irritating caring for trivia which is a courtier's life: at what precise time should His Majesty arrive at the Cathedral for the Easter Sunday mass? How big should his cortège be? Should the Queen Mother—while still in mourning—come to what was a religious festival of joy?

We pondered such problems and prepared our own uniforms and medals: we looked like garish hotel doormen with the gold braid down our dress trousers, the decorations jangling on our chests that were boiling inside our starched shirtfronts, while our necks were chafed by the stiff wing collars.

On the night of Easter Saturday, the square of the Metropolis—the cathedral—was jammed with people who all cheered suitably. In the church, the Soviet ambassador, in full uniform, displayed a galaxy of stars on his militaristic tunic. He stood and sat at all the right moments in the service—he came from an Orthdox country, after all. I swear I heard him sing snatches of the resurrection hymn.

When the service was over, we came out into the square and the Metropolitan archbishop of Athens lighted the King's candle, shouting 'Christ is risen' and the crowd roared 'truly He is risen'. The King lighted candles around him, from his own—we all carried them—and the flame spread, lighting smiling eyes. There was, around us, the buzz of a contented crowd. Svelte and handsome in his uniform of air marshal, with the sash of the highest order in Greece and the collar of Denmark's Order of the Elephant, the King was cheered lustily. There was evident affection and goodwill in the voices of the crowd. This felt like a new, a clean beginning. I still was not aware that important events were about to test the freedom of my country.

Despite the continuing mourning for the King's father, the court lived in a state of suppressed festiveness because we were all immersed in the preparations for the wedding of King Constantine with Princess Anne-Marie of Denmark. They were both very young and very much in love. It was the stuff of fairy tales and no one—however old and cynical—ever frees himself from the spell of fairy tales.

There was precise planning by the Master of Ceremonies and the military household of the King: the timetable of the various happenings was expressed in seconds: 'at 10 hours, 27 minutes, 35 seconds, the King of Denmark enters the cathedral . . .' Working back from that time, the precise second at which the King of Denmark would be at certain points along the ceremonial route was calculated. At those points there would be parade marshals, equipped with walkie-talkies and detailed timetables and they would signal each driver to accelerate or decelerate so that each of the august visitors—kings, heads of state—would enter the cathedral at the prescribed time.

Security along the route would be intense. All buildings would be searched; all people in those buildings would have to be approved by the police; all suspicious objects examined. There were possible targets for the assassins: Palestinian guerrillas were threatening to kill the King of Jordan, for instance.

Housekeeping arrangements were difficult. The best hoteliers in Greece came to the court, begging not to have their establishments designated as residences for any of the royal guests: 'At the wedding of Princess Sophia, the King's sister, two years ago, you assigned several floors of our hotel to royal guests. They kept our staff working all night, ran up enormous hotel bills and never paid—they never even tipped. Please spare us.'

The jewellers presented another problem. One of them had been given the task of producing a strictly limited number of silver 'bonbonnières' at the time of Princess Sophia's wedding. Only heads of state and royal guests would receive these commemorative silver boxes. The jeweller produced boxes in their thousands and sold them as souvenirs to tourists. I found it impossible to have this jeweller struck from the list of suppliers to the palace: he had a protector at the palace, a protector who had shared in the profits from the sale of the bonbonnières. Everyone knew about this in Athens and the story generated a good deal of criticism among the public.

Then, also, there was the matter of presents. Every worker in the government and the armed forces was forced to contribute towards the wedding gifts. Greece is a poor country with a low standard of living. Taxing lowly clerks to buy forty-eight place settings in solid gold was clumsy. Goodwill for the young King diminished visibly.

I was disquieted by such evidence that the palace was not sufficiently sensitive to the currents of sentiment in the country. When I spoke up about this, most of the other courtiers would say: 'Nonsense. His Majesty is adored. All he needs do is walk out among his people and the people will prove by their adoration that all these things you worry about do not matter.' The courtiers would say the same thing to the King himself and to the King's mother.

Even when the royal motorcade—going at 100 miles an hour—knocked down an old man and broke his leg, most courtiers dismissed the accident as unimportant. The fact that such accidents had occurred quite frequently in the past—the King's father also loved speed—did not seem to make an impression at the palace. The King visited the old man who had been knocked down. The courtiers were ecstatic:

'Wasn't that generous of His Majesty? Imagine, the King himself went to see this old workman at the hospital. And His Majesty ordered that the workman's family should want for nothing this Easter. A beautiful hamper will be sent, with all sorts of goodies. How marvellous of the King! Now that's what the press should be writing about.'

Then there was the invitation list. A supper would be served on the eve of the royal wedding. Apart from the crowned heads and heads of state, only 'Athens society' was to be invited to the supper. The nominal list of Athens society included several people who had become rich in dubious ways—a shipowner, for example, who had made a fortune transporting Jewish refugees to Palestine in ships that had been sold for scrap iron and which had no facilities of any kind on board; refugees by the hundreds had suffered in these plague ships. There were several traitors on the 'Athens society' list—men and women who had collaborated with the Nazis in World War Two. Left off the list were many good artists, writers, prominent professors, winners of Greece's highest decoration for bravery. There even were, on the society list, two men who had attempted to assassinate Eleutherios Venizelos, the great liberal statesman of Greece.

70

Those of us who were called 'the red courtiers' won the battle of the invitations: at afternoon garden parties before the wedding, the people of Greece who had served in their fields with excellence were invited: nurses who had worked in advanced hospitals in the country's many wars; the heroes of those wars; the firemen with the best record of courage; school teachers who had volunteered to work in the backwoods and had brought learning to the shepherd boys; priests who had been true spiritual leaders of their threatened villages through all the perils of the land.

'My dear young friend,' said General Constantine Dovas, head of the King's military household, 'your point of view is admirably populist but think of the country's prestige. Think of the smell! Imagine exposing the King's bride to such rabble.'

'That rabble, general, are the citizens of our democracy,' I said, feeling pompous but too angry to keep quiet.

'I used the word rabble as a jocular exaggeration, of course,' said General Dovas. 'I am a man of the people myself. But that does not mean we should go too far in our concessions to the people. We have done that too often. Our parliamentarians do that too often: they play up to the mob and that is why our democracy is such a mess.'

'What alternative to Parliament do you propose?' I asked, 'dictatorship?'

'Goodness no! Dictators are so tiresome. If we must have a Parliament, and I suppose we must, let us reduce its capacity for mischief. We should have something like the American system; only ours would be better because we would not have to elect a president.'

'You mean you would want the King to have the powers that an American president has.'

'Precisely, my dear Secretary General. The executive and the legislative should be separated. The King would appoint ministers from among the best people in the land and not from Parliament.'

'And what would Parliament do?' I asked.

'It would approve or disapprove the legislation proposed by the King's ministers. There should be limits, of course, to how much disapproving our indescribable representatives of the rabble could do.'

'You mean we should ask Parliament to divest itself of its powers?'

'We won't ask them, we'll tell them,' said General Dovas.

I had heard the argument before—in terms less insulting to Parliament; I had heard it from the Queen Mother. I broached the matter to the King and found that he himself favoured a constitution along US presidential lines, with himself in the role of president. The fact that he would not be elected but would be chief executive by divine right and heredity, did not seem to strike His Majesty as odd.

What I heard worried me a great deal. I decided to explore the matter further, to pump General Dovas. I chose him because he was quite naive in his anti-communism and had, therefore, an inordinate admiration for my resistance to brainwashing in Korea. I also chose him because he was a general and I had found generals easy to pump. I remember, for instance, wanting some information from General Nathan Twining, when he had been Chairman of the US Joint Chiefs of Staff and I had been Washington correspondent for the London *Observer*. Britain's minister of defence had just visited Washington and had announced with great fanfare that he was acquiring an American rocket called the Sky Bolt, to be launched from his country's obsolete bomber fleet. This American rocket, the minister had said, would prolong the life of the bomber fleet and give Britain a fine deterrent force.

I had heard from minor sources that there was something wrong with the deal and I wanted to check this with General Twining. It was a Friday and I needed the information very quickly to meet my deadline in London. Fortunately, both General Twining and I were attending the same dinner party. My hostess had a very pretty and humorous daughter who was a good friend. I asked her to pump General Twining for me and briefed her on what I wanted.

So she told the general that she worried about war with Russia and worried that Washington was giving away to Britain those Sky Bolt rockets instead of keeping them to defend the US. We were at the coffee and liqueur stage and General Twining was in an expansive and florid mood.

'Don't you worry your pretty head, little girl,' he said, stroking her thigh, 'don't you worry at all. We can blast the Russians off the face of the earth and we'll do so before they can touch us.'

'But we're giving away our rockets,' she said, 'and that frightens me.'

'We're giving away scrap,' said the worthy general who by

now was getting bolder with his gestures. 'Scrap, like the Bomarc rockets we gave Canada and they're not good for anything. As for the Sky Bolt, we're not even going to manufacture them. They're not worth a damn.'

'But the British minister said . . .'

'He's a politician, little girl. He needs to say something right now, so he says we'll sell him the Sky Bolt.'

'Does he know you won't manufacture it?' the girl asked.

'Let's say he's got a shrewd idea. But let's not talk about this sort of thing. I want to talk about you . . .' In the event, the Sky Bolt was never manufactured nor, of course, delivered to Britain.

So, I had learned from experience that generals are easy to pump and I pumped General Dovas.

It was done casually, in snatches of conversation, under the guise of discussing news items, especially those that made parliamentarians round the world appear in a bad light or items illustrating the danger of Communist takeovers in various parts of the world.

Dovas was obsessed by the fear that the Greek Liberal government then in power would interfere with the armed forces and try to place Liberals in positions of control.

Did I consider it right for politicians to mix themselves in the affairs of the army and choose officers for command on grounds of political ideology rather than on grounds of loyalty and competence? he would ask.

I could safely say that I did not think such a procedure right and this further endeared me to General Dovas. I knew, of course, that as caretaker prime minister, appointed by the late King Paul to run the 1961 elections, General Dovas had used the army to stuff ballot boxes to keep out those he considered disloyal. In one village in Crete, for instance, the royalist candidate had received many more votes than there were voters.[4]

Dovas considered the Prime Minister, George Papandreou, a Communist: Papandreou had once called a party he led 'socialist' and for Dovas Socialism and Communism were identical.

'Didn't Kerensky usher in the Communists in Russia?' Dovas asked.

I did not dispute him. I wanted to find out whether he was merely expressing opinions or whether he was preparing something. At times I had to remind myself of Dovas' role in the 1961 elections, so unlike a sinister conspirator did he look; he was a short, rumpled man, with a limp and a pink, balding smiling face, much like that of the more cheerful of Snowhite's seven dwarfs.

But while smiling benevolently, he could talk of dark plots which he conjectured were being prepared by the Liberals: Would it not be reasonable, from the Liberals' point of view, now that they have a majority in Parliament, to prepare a coup and replace all the loyal officers by their own men, Dovas would ask? Especially when the son of the Prime Minister is a Communist?

'A Communist, Andreas Papandreou?' I was astonished.

'He has a police dossier. He was a member of a Trotskyist organisation.'

Andreas Papandreou, when a young student, had opposed the Fascist dictatorship which ruled Greece in the 1930's, had been arrested by the police and labelled a 'Trotskyist' as were all those so arrested. It was enough to write 'down with dictatorship' on a tempting white wall to acquire a dossier as a Trostkyist.

I encouraged General Dovas to come back on his conspiracy theme:

'I don't believe in coups,' I said. 'I hope measures have been taken to make sure no coup takes place.'

'We've taken measures,' said Dovas, smiling. 'We have seen to it that loyal officers hold key positions.'

Through the days I saw some officers visit Dovas often. He was head of the King's military household and visits to him by officers were normal but I still felt I was on the trail of something.

Finding out the names of such officers was not very hard: it meant asking a valet: 'That officer who entered General Dovas' office—my father showed him to me once and told me he was remarkable, I've forgotten his name . . .' Or 'I met that officer at a party the other evening and promised to send him a newspaper clipping and I've forgotten his name . . .'

So I got my list of names, George Papadopoulos, Michael Roufogallis, John Ladas, Nicolas Makarezos, Demetrios Ioannides, Demetrios Balopoulos, Stylianos Pattakos: later they were the junta.

The contingent of gendarmes who guarded the palace had a sergeant major who was getting married. He sent invitations to all the courtiers. I was the only one to give him a wedding present and he became a great admirer of mine. I would occasionally drop in by his little lodge where a register was kept of all visitors

74

to the palace, giving the names of whom they were visiting, and the hours of the visits.

I also was quite friendly with Major Michael Arnaoutis, private secretary to the King. On four separate occasions, while I was in his office, he received telephone calls from someone he addressed as 'Mr Chief', presumably the chief of the General Staff. I stood to go but Arnaoutis motioned me, politely, to remain. These telephone conversations were more cryptic than his usual ones. They obviously concerned the desire 'of the palace' to have certain persons appointed in certain positions. Major Arnaoutis referred to these persons by their Christian names. It happened that these were the Christian names of General Dovas' frequent visitors.

It was flimsy evidence but I gave it to my father who said he would see what he could do with it. 'That "Nasser" Papadopoulos visits the palace is significant,' father said. 'That fellow has been plotting for years, presumably against the day when the Liberals would be in power. Keep your eyes and ears open and I shall see what I can dig up.'

The next day, all my time and thinking was taken up with ceremony. Princess Anne Marie and her attendants were arriving in Athens. We all went to the airport in uniforms or morning coats. I felt silly in my top hat—I had never worn one before.

Princess Anne Marie was very tense. On closer inspection, she looked petrified, especially in contrast to the other ladies from the Danish court who were very relaxed and chatty, enjoying the sunshine and happily aware of the hungry looks they attracted from the tall evzones of the royal guard.

The ceremonial went off without a hitch. The timing was perfect—even though my toy poodle fought battles with the pompons on the boots of the Royal Guards who were trying to stand at rigid attention.

Shortly thereafter we flew to Salonika where the King was to break ground for a new industrial development. I watched, with unease, personages who were suspected of being implicated in the assassination of a left-wing member of Parliament, Gregory Lambrakis whose death was the subject of the famous movie 'Z' by Costa Gavras. These suspects talked freely with the King and he seemed to be on good terms with them. That night, back in Athens, a visitor had wanted to eat and to break dishes and it fell to me to play host.

'Call me George,'[5] said the visitor. 'I am travelling incognito. Have I told you about my new car?'

I listened to his talk about carburettors, cams, differentials and other innards of the car. I ordered food and asked that we be interrupted frequently by the bouzouki band which was to serenade George—that would provide pauses in his talk about cars. I also ordered dishes.

'How many, Mr General?' asked the tavern owner.

'As many as you can spare. The gentleman, here, wants to break dishes.'

'His presence honours us . . .'

'He wants to remain incognito,' I said firmly. 'Do you have anyone who speaks English and knows about cars?'

'There is a taxi at the stand on the corner. The driver owns the car and is always talking about it. He speaks English.'

'Tell him I'll rent him by the hour and would he please join us for supper. What's his name?'

'Vangellis. I'll go fetch him.'

George, and the taxi driver Vangellis, spent a happy night together discussing transmissions, gears, alternators: rather, George talked and Vangellis gave all the right responses, as in a religious service.

'I have eight cylinders,' said George.

'Bravo, George,' said Vangellis. 'I always say eight cylinders, bravo.'

'And four carburettors.'

'Holy Virgin, mother of God! Four carburettors!'

'With pressurised injection, in phased ratios,' said George, or at least, that's what I thought he said.

'Po po po,' said Vangellis which is Greek for Ooh la la.

The Bouzouki band, at regular intervals, bent over George and serenaded him with the current Athenian love songs. George smiled shyly, embarrassed but obviously pleased.

'The independent suspension has special shock absorbers and I can do a ninety degree turn at ninety miles an hour.'

'Ninety miles an hour! One hundred and forty-four kilometres. My little Jesus, lend a hand,' said Vangellis, ecstatic.

We also broke dishes, George would pick them from the dozen proffered him by the waiter and let them drop one by one on the floor. Another waiter would bring another dozen while a third swept up. George was generous: he wanted Vangellis and me to break plates also. Inevitably, I over-ate as I always do when I haven't anything more important to do. We left at four in the morning because the tavern had run out of spare plates. I put George in the official car with the bodyguard who was quite upset at having to take Vangellis along—George would not part with his new-found friend. And I walked home through the streets of Plaka, at the foot of the Acropolis.

Someone suddenly stood in front of me and spat in my face. In reflexive anger I brought my knee up into his groin and brought it up again to catch his jaw as he bent from the agony of the first blow. I twisted his arm behind his back. Already I was beginning to feel sorry I had been so violent.

'Look,' I said. 'I am sorry I had to hit you, but you started it.'

'Dirty traitor,' said the man as he was still gasping for breath.

'You have mistaken me for someone else.'

'No I have not, *Mister* Secretary-General, the newest traitor in town.'

'I haven't betrayed you. I don't even know you.'

'You wouldn't admit to knowing me. Arse-licking courtiers don't admit they know ordinary people, do they, *Mister* Secretary-General? But when you needed us you weren't so stand-offish. You were all smiles. When my mother hears of this, she'll curse the day she ever gave you shortbread when your father was in jail.'

I let go his hand. I spoke his name—let us say it was Manoli.[6] His mother had indeed given me shortbread when my father had been put in jail by the Fascists.

'I'm sorry, Manoli. I didn't recognise you. I wouldn't have hit you, otherwise.'

'I recognised you. That's why I spat at you.'

'But why?'

'Let's not play-act,' said Manoli.

'I am not play-acting. I give you my word of honour I do not know what I have done that may have made you spit at me.'

'I'm going,' he said. 'You make me more disgusted every minute.'

I was beginning to get angry again: 'You spit at a man,' I said, 'you call him a traitor and that's all? If you're a man speak up. What's eating you?'

'You want to know? Do you really want to know what's eating me? Then come along.'

77

He was sobbing as he ran. I knew where he was going. I had been to his home so many times when I had been small. It was only a few streets away. The door was open when I got there.

His mother met me. She was civil with the civility of the proud when they are frightened. She had never been like that with me before.

'In here,' Manoli said.

I walked into the next room.

'That's Katina,' the mother said. She was the baby. She had been eighteen months old when I had last seen her, mischievous and giggly with velvety black eyes that made her the darling of the neighbourhood. And now she was a woman sitting on the floor, holding her knees to her chest and rocking back and forth. Tears were streaming down her face. There was snot on her upper lip. Her mother wiped with a handkerchief, chiding her as if speaking to a child. The room smelled of urine, which obviously embarrassed the mother.

'The hair that is missing was pulled out,' said Manoli. 'They left some hair. If you want to stay till she has one of her fits she'll tell you herself what they did to her. She'll tell you why her feet are in plaster; they broke them, beating her on her soles with crow-bars. To stifle her cries they used a gag dipped in excrement. She'd vomit and nearly drown on her vomit. Before that, while she was still clean, they raped her. That's what your fine friends did to her.'

'Please, Manoli,' I said. 'Don't speak in riddles. Who did this to her?'

'The people with whom you were photographed in Salonika, you traitor: they had it done to her.'

'Hush, Manoli,' said the mother, weeping, 'don't speak like that. It's lacking in respect. You can't talk like that to the King's Secretary General.' She was extremely nervous, wiping her hands compulsively on her apron.

'It doesn't matter how I talk to him, mother. I've already spat in his face. And he has already begun giving me a beating.'

Manoli's mother burst into tears: 'Oh my God,' she said, 'intervene my God. Protect us. Mr Secretary General, forgive my son. You know how he is. It's that terrible temper of his but he is a good man and a loyal man. He obeys the law and has never voted against any government. Please have pity. Don't take Manoli away. He is the only support I have now that Katina is like this. And she may well stay like this. Please have pity.' She sobbed loudly, her mouth fully opened. She had given herself over to her grief. The upper part of her dentures came loose and she did nothing about it. In between her sobs she kept saying: 'God, I am so frightened, I am so frightened. Dear mother of God, intervene.'

I remember feeling rage at the fact that this poor woman was genuinely frightened of me.

'Look,' I said. 'I have only just come to Greece after being away for very many years. I didn't know this sort of thing was going on. I would never be associated with this kind of brutality.'

'But you are,' said Manoli, 'and don't give us this crap about not knowing what was going on here. Aren't you supposed to be a journalist? Aren't you the one who always dug up the facts when the government wanted to keep them hidden? You didn't know! That's too easy a way out, *Mister* Secretary General.'

'I didn't know, I tell you. I didn't know.'

'You knew. You knew. You were beaten by the police when you were eleven.'

'I thought this sort of thing had stopped.'

'Don't lie, you filthy bastard.' He was trembling with rage, his eyes cloudy, his lips half open, saliva running out at each corner, down to his shirt whose collar was stained by sweat. 'There have been stories in the papers about torture in our jails, you bastard,' said Manoli. 'Don't pretend you did not know.'

'They were Communist stories, Manoli.'

'Not all Communist stories are untrue. Didn't you care enough to find out whether they were true or not?'

'I thought this sort of thing had stopped with the civil war.'

'You mean you wanted to think it had stopped so that your conscience wouldn't hurt you when you accepted to work at the palace, *Mister* Secretary General.'

'I'm sorry, Manoli.'

'What bloody good does it do that you are sorry?' He started sobbing, like his mother. 'You'll be sorry a few minutes, then you'll go back to wearing your top hat and tails and going out to break plates. I never thought you would end up as a court jester.'

'Is there anything I can do?'

'Yes, you can get out,' said Manoli. 'You're dirtying our house. Get out, you louse.'

I turned to his mother. 'Please believe me,' I said. 'I didn't know this sort of thing was going on. I am very sorry. Won't you please tell me what happened, why this happened?'

'I don't know why,' said the mother. 'One day she did not come back from work. We looked for her. I asked the police where she was. We put announcements in the papers. She was found in the streets by some friends last week. She had been away a month. Now she doesn't talk to us. She doesn't talk at all except when she has her fits and then she screams. She begs for mercy. She says "not the gag with the excrement, no, no". At other times she says, "please don't hit my feet any more, please". I went to fetch a policeman so he could see what had happened to my daughter. When she saw him she screamed worse than ever . . .'

'So you don't really know who did this to her, I mean which people, specifically.'

'Are you trying to tell me the police are not guilty?' said Manoli.

'No, I'm not trying to tell you that. But if I am going to do something about it, I must have more precise information than what you have given me. Whoever did this must be punished. I need all the information you can give me.'

'You're not going to do anything.'

'Why not, Manoli?'

'Because you have a nice fat job as Secretary General, and you will not do anything that endangers your job.'

'I have another job waiting for me in America. I can leave this job any time.'

'You want me to believe you do not care about this job?'

'I didn't say that. All I said was that if I lost this job, I had another waiting for me.'

'Maybe you should not do anything,' said Manoli's mother. 'These men who did this to my daughter would stop at nothing. If you do anything, Mr Secretary General, they might come to get my son because he told you what happened.'

'They might come to get you too, *Mister* Secretary General. You wouldn't like that, would you?' said Manoli.

'No. I wouldn't. I shall be careful.'

'I know, I know. Nothing must happen to *you*, Mr Secretary General, must it?'

'Nor to you Manoli. If your mother is right, these men would take it out on you for having talked to me. For all we know, I was followed and they saw what happened. Maybe they will arrest you after I walk out.' The minute I had spoken the words, I wished I had remained silent for Manoli's mother began sobbing with fear again.

'I have nothing to lose,' Manoli said. 'I'll tell you all I know.'

'No my son, don't talk, please don't talk. You must talk to no one. You know what happened to the son of the lady in the other street. He talked and we haven't seen him since.'

'I have talked enough, already Mother. It's too late to worry whether we can trust him. He knows enough to denounce me and you so I lose nothing.'

'You have nothing to fear from me,' I said. 'All I want is to help you.'

'I'll tell you all I know and you can denounce me if you like,' Manoli said. 'I won't let them catch me alive.' I looked at him. He was not the fighting type—I could not imagine him fighting a last ditch against policemen come to capture him. But neither was Manoli a man who ever talked idly. He continued talking in a dull voice against the background of his mother's quiet sobs and the almost continuous whine that was the only sound Katina made. 'Katina's fiancé was a follower of Lambrakis, Gregory Lambrakis the member of Parliament whom they assassinated; the one they called Communist but he was not Communist, neither was Stavro, Katina's intended. Stavro had been in Salonika on the day of the assassination—it was in Salonika that they killed Lambrakis. Stavro never talked about the assassination to us or to Katina. We were curious: we asked Katina if Stavros had said anything to her. When Katina disappeared, I went to find Stavro. Maybe he knew where she was, I told myself. Maybe they have jumped the gun, those two, and are already living together before the marriage and Katina doesn't dare tell mother : Katina is not a young girl any more. She and Stavro have been saving for years to buy themselves a small apartment. It's been slow—a secretary and an accountant can't save much from their salaries. No one had seen Stavro at his room for a week; his things were still there. I went to where he worked. They had not seen him either and they were angry. They said they were going to fire him. Three days later a policeman told Stavro's people that he had been run over by a car and that they could claim the body at the morgue.'

'Is that all?' I asked.

'What more do you want? The fingerprints of the men who killed Stavro and who tortured my sister?'

'Look, Manoli, it all seems to mean what you think it means, but it isn't the sort of evidence that would stand up in a court of law. Did the police say who drove the car that killed Stavro?'

'They said it had been a hit and run accident.'

'Do you see what I mean? We can't prove anything.'

'It isn't a question of proving guilt. It is a case of wanting to clean out the bastards who do these things. Take away from them the power to do such things,' said Manoli, 'and you will have a hundred witnesses who are too scared to talk now.'

'One would have to have reasons to suspend these men from duty,' I said.

'Everyone knows what they do. Go see for yourself. You know where their headquarters are. You'll find at least six of them outside revving up motorcycles to drown out the screaming inside.'

'That's an old story. They used to do that before the war.'

'They still do it.'

'But don't you see, Manoli, how easily they could deny they did anything wrong? They are revving up motorcycles. It's noisy, but is it a crime? You think they killed Stavro, but there are no witnesses. You say they tortured Katina, but she is out of her mind. She couldn't testify.'

'So you have a whole set of excuses for doing nothing. Why did you bother asking us questions? Go, damn you. Get out.'

'I was hoping you might have more evidence, witnesses.'

'If you leave those monsters alone, there will be no witnesses. Look what they did to Stavro.'

'You believe they killed him. I may believe they killed him. That does not constitute evidence.'

'And the people who allegedly commit suicide by jumping out of windows at the headquarters of the security police? Isn't that evidence?'

'Have you seen them jump, Manoli? Has anyone seen them? How do you know they jumped from that building?'

'People have seen them jump; there are witnesses but they either are afraid to talk or they think it is right and proper for the state to beat people up and to throw them out of windows.'

We got nowhere, Manoli and I.

Back at my hotel, I was called by the palace switchboard: 'You must leave us telephone numbers where you can be reached at all times, Mr General.

'I do, don't I?'

'Not last night, Mr General.'

'Sure I did. I went to a tavern and phoned you from there.'

'But after the tavern, Mr General.'

'Well, it was a beautiful night and I stayed out till the dawn. But how do you know I didn't go home right away?'

'We called you. You were not there, Mr General.'

'Why did you call me?'

'There was an overseas phone call for you. We told them to call back in a few minutes and we would try to locate you.'

'Why didn't you simply tell them to call my hotel?'

'We didn't know whether you would want to take the call, Mr General.'

'Why, who was calling?'

'They didn't say.'

'Then how did you know I might not want to take the call?'

'Forgive me, Mr General, but my lines are buzzing.'

I told myself I should not give in to paranoia and begin suspecting that the palace switchboard tried to reach me because I had sent the driver of the official car away with 'George' early that morning.

And what could I do about Katina? Was Stavros, her fiancé, silenced because he had witnessed something connected with the murder of Gregory Lambrakis? Had the police interrogated Katina to find out whether Stavro had talked to her? Paranoia?

I tried to put Katina out of my mind: there was much work to do on the Cyprus issue. The Duke of Edinburgh had told King Constantine that Greece's case over Cyprus was not sufficiently well put and that an information campaign was urgent. The King had asked me what I thought could be done to put the Greek case across.

In 1964, while I was working for the King of Greece, Turkey was preparing to land on Cyprus. I had no doubt in my mind, in view of the Turkish record, that the chances of a massacre by Turkish troops were extremely high.[7] I was also afraid that under the terror of a Turkish invasion, the worst elements among the Greek Cypriots might also commit unacceptable acts. Our problem was to convince the Americans that they should exert maximum pressure against any Turkish landing on Cyprus. The Turks were exercising counter-pressure on Washington, threatening that they would leave NATO or that they would deny the use of their territory to America's forces.

I produced a plan of action and the King asked me to show it to Prime Minister George Papandreou. The Prime Minister asked me to discuss the plan with his son Andreas who was a Cabinet Minister and who had worked in the US, as an economist, for many years.

From our very first meeting, I liked Andreas Papandreou. He had a brilliant mind and a good heart. I trusted him and it was obvious he trusted me. We met frequently and this was duly noted at the palace. The King asked me about my meetings with Andreas and I reported on the work Andreas and I had done to put together the information campaign with which we hoped to restrain Turkish bellicosity. His Majesty did not comment. The next day, I was summoned to see Her Majesty, Queen Frederika, the Queen Mother.

Queen Frederika wanted to know how I found Andreas Papandreou. I said I liked him a great deal. But how did I find his politics, I was asked. I said that some of the policies Andreas had in mind seemed long overdue : modernising the economy; bringing in foreign capital on terms fair to Greece; raising the standard of living of the poorer classes so as to increase their purchasing power, and so on.

But he planned to increase trade with the Communist bloc, said the Queen, did I agree? I replied that there was a spirit of détente in the world. NATO countries are talking of discussing economic co-operation with the Soviet bloc.

'Do you agree?'

'With détente, in general, yes, I agree. Your Majesty.'

The Queen allowed me to take my leave. Next, I had a visit from Major Michael Arnaoutis, the King's private secretary. He inquired after my health and I after his and his wife's health—she was ailing.

He remarked that I had had the privilege of talking to the King. I admitted that this was so and further admitted that I had had the privilege of a conversation with the Queen Mother.

'What did you say to the Queen?' the major asked.

I told him.

I had been away a long time, the major said, and was obviously not aware of some things that had been happening. The Queen had been persecuted and insulted over Ambatielos, the imprisoned Communist. Ambatielos's wife picketed the Queen abroad. Ambatielos had been properly tried. He had been found guilty as charged and now because of a clever public relations campaign, we were being asked to release him. It was all too easy to forget that these Communist prisoners had been convicted under criminal law, for common crimes, like complicity in murder, conspiracy to murder, being accessory before and after the fact. They were not political prisoners. They were common criminals.

Were all these Communist prisoners murderers or accessories, I asked.

No. There were some who were caught armed, while they were fighting to overthrow the state. No state accepts that. These Communists were even prepared to give up part of the state—to give part of Macedonia to the Bulgarians.

I said I knew that the Greek Communist Party had supported the claims of the Bulgarians on Macedonia—like most Greeks I reject such claims and believe they are baseless.

It was upsetting to the men in the armed forces, Major Arnaoutis said, to hear talk of freeing the Communists who were prepared to give up part of Greece and who were responsible for massacres and destruction and assassination.

I said I could see that this sort of thing would be upsetting. We could not leave assassins unpunished. But we should be consistent: we should punish the assassins of Gregory Lambrakis.

'Yes we must,' said Major Arnaoutis. 'And, oh, it would be a good idea if you went to visit Mr Panayotis Pipinelis. He is a first rate political thinker. His Majesty the King admires Mr Pipinelis a great deal.'

I didn't follow the advice immediately. In the course of the next few days, nearly every courtier asked me whether I had made arrangements to see Mr Pipinelis. It was obvious that this meeting was important to the royal family and its courtiers. So I found myself in the living-room of Mr Pipinelis' seaside villa. At our one previous meeting, he had been in his office as the permanent under-secretary for external affairs. He had sat, then, in a chair whose seat was a good four inches higher than any other in the room. And he had had a stool to keep his feet from dangling. Mr Pipinelis was excessively short and obviously unhappy about his lack of inches.

'I am glad you came to see me,' he said.

'It is an honour to see you, Mr President'—Mr Pipinelis had headed a short-lived caretaker government and was therefore entitled to the courtesy title of *President*. We sat informally on wicker armchairs and sipped lemonade.

He expressed pleasure at my being in the palace and complimented me on being a liberal man, but not naive.

I said I strove not to be naive.

That I accepted to serve in the palace was a sign that I was a realist, said Mr Pipinelis. He assumed that I would not have accepted to work for the King if I did not believe in the viability of the Greek royal house. Mr Pipinelis leaned forward in his chair and fixed me with his pale eyes as if he were trying to read my innermost thoughts.

Under the right conditions, I said, the Royal House was viable.

The Royal House could give Greece stability, said Mr Pipinelis, which was what the country needed most of all. Did I realise that between 1897 and 1947, in fifty years, Greece had twenty-five years of war or revolution? That was an enormous drain on the energy and genius of the nation. Greeks could produce a third civilisation if they did not spend their genius on fighting.

The 'third Greek civilisation' had been a slogan of the Fascist régime before the Second World War. Pipinelis had been a partisan of that régime in his various diplomatic posts: a more zealous advocate than a diplomat needs to be. He sat in his chair, gnome-like, pale, fixing me with his eyes as if to mesmerise me. It was quite evident that Mr Pipinelis was intent upon converting me. I did not want him to feel he was not succeeding— not until I had heard him out, at least. I soon realised that not much dissembling was required: Mr Pipinelis had a firm belief in his powers of conversion. Each time I nodded in mere politeness, he looked triumphant, like an old and vain guru who takes his chela through the steps leading to enlightenment.

The Greeks, he said, could not afford uncertainty any more. We were a small nation with few resources. To achieve our destiny we needed continuity. In politics, only the Royal House could provide such continuity. Our political parties could not. They were agglomerations of personal fiefdoms with no fixed ideological line. Which was just as well because we could not afford real ideological divisions. Greeks tend to become too passionate about ideology and destroy one another. That was why, the executive power must be in the hands of the King. He should appoint the Cabinet which should be accountable only to him; and the elected Parliament should have only a limited power to veto decisions of the executive. In fact, we should have a presidential constitution, as in the United States; ours would be more stable, however, because we would not have an elected president but a King. Thus, our executive would be able to be far-sighted in its planning because it would not have to worry about winning elections. At the end of this peroration, Mr Pipinelis made it clear that an answer was expected of me : he bent forward, turning his ear towards me; his cupped hand did not quite touch the ear, but the pose was unmistakable. Out of the corner of his eyes he was transfixing me with a commanding stare.

What if we were afflicted with an incompetent King, I asked, or one who was mentally deranged—like George the third, of England?

Mr Pipinelis couldn't have been more delighted : my question, obviously, had been the one he had prepared for in his mind : in the modern world, he explained, the King, in the sort of system Mr Pipinelis envisaged, would not have the power George the third had had. He would have a cabinet of recognised experts. His army staff—and we had a strong standing army in Greece, with properly professional officers—would contain the possible errors of a king who was not up to his task.

So the real power would be in the hands of the king's advisers. Was that what Mr Pipinelis proposed?

Only if the King was not up to his task. Only then would his advisers contain the King.

But an incompetent king might appoint incompetent advisers, I objected.

There would be arrangements to make that impossible.

'What arrangements?'

Co-optive arrangements, Mr Pipinelis said. The King's advisers would see that their eventual successors were carefully selected, carefully trained. There would be a career progression which would filter out the unsuitable gradually so that those who reached the top—those who made it to the eligibility list from which the King would choose his advisers—would be the best.

'Plato's Republic,' I said.

Mr Pipinelis exuded gratification : he clasped his hands together and did his best to repress a laugh so that his throat swelled, emitting a sound not unlike the gobble of a turkey. The noise ended and Mr Pipinelis was, at last, able to speak : I flattered him when I compared his ideas with Plato's, he said,

87

delightedly. Yes, a platonic elite would make the country great.

I felt that I was involved in a grotesque farce. Was this man simply pulling my leg? Was I having delusions? But no, the pale gnome before me continued his lecture:

A co-optive elite of civilians and soldiers serving the higher purpose of the state, that's what we needed, said Pipinelis; that was his modern platonism, to serve the higher purpose.

'Which higher purpose, Mr Pipinelis?'

'The protection of the true national values.'

'As defined by whom?'

'As defined by history.'

'Could you give me an example?'

'But you learned all these things at school, my dear young friend. You remember the oath of the ancient Greek youths when they began their military service:

"I shall not shame my weapons, nor abandon my comrades in arms. I shall fight for what we hold holy and sacred, alone or in a group. I shall not hand over a lesser fatherland than I received. And I shall abide by our laws that exist as well as those that will be wisely promulgated. And I shall not allow anyone to overturn or disobey the laws: I shall defend these along with others, or even alone. I shall honour what was sacred to our fathers. Let the gods Agraulos, Enyalios, Ares, Zeus, Thallo, Auxo and Hegemone be witnesses".'[8]

He declaimed the words of the oath, his right arm stretched forward, palm down—for that was how the ancient Greeks swore. As Mr Pipinelis spoke, he seemed to be in a trance. When he had finished declaiming, he remained silent. When he looked at me again, his expression had changed.

'You seem displeased,' he said. ' I might even says you look disgusted.'

I had been thinking of Katina, sitting on the floor in her shabby room, her scalp stripped of hair here and there, her eyes vacant, rocking back and forth holding her knees to her breasts and whining a whine of terror.

'Would you mind telling me why you look disgusted?' Mr Pipinelis asked.

I said I had been thinking of what could happen to a human being in prison.

Ah yes, my unfortunate experiences as a prisoner of war in Korea. Mr Pipinelis had read my book. I was the sort of man of whose anti-Communist loyalties there could be no doubt—I had seen Communists in their true colours. Then Pipinelis' tone changed : I had been very inquisitive. I had been very observant. Some felt I had been too inquisitive. Mr Pipinelis preferred to assume I had not been prying but trying, so to speak, to initiate myself into the mysteries. That was the interpretation Pipinelis had been giving to my actions. It would be dangerous for me, and my family, if Pipinelis' interpretation was wrong. Would I like some more lemonade?

'There are things that trouble me,' I said, 'like the murder of Lambrakis, the member of Parliament.'

I was clearly going too far, said Mr Pipinelis. Just because a man who insulted the Queen was killed was no reason to be upset. Lambrakis put himself beyond the pale. He did not belong to the grand design. It could hardly matter that he was eliminated. In fact it would have mattered if he had not been eliminated. Why should we persecute loyal officers on the grounds that they had something to do with the elimination of vermin?

Again I asked myself whether this scene was real or whether I was dreaming. But no, I was there and Pipinelis was there, still talking :

The best system for Greece was a system of loyalty. I was a natural candidate for membership in that system, as Secretary General to the King. Pipinelis was sure I would be loyal and, in consequence, the system would be loyal to me. Here Mr Pipinelis paused again and fixed me with his eye. He was giving a last chance and he was putting all his will into it : it might not be long before this current phase of our 'so-called parliamentary democracy' ended for ever, to be replaced by a system such as the one Pipinelis proposed. In such a change, he would expect to see my loyalty rewarded and it doubtlessly would be. 'I see you as a Cabinet Minister soon. You have admirable qualifications for many cabinet posts. I have not forgotten your naval background. You were first in your class. You may well be the man to be Minister of the Navy.' Or Minister of Information. Or Foreign Minister. Not immediately : I would be given time to acquire the necessary experience, as a junior minister, working for a senior minister. He stopped and examined me carefully to see what effect he was having on me. It was not a perfunctory examination : he leaned forward and focused on one of my eyes then on the other. He cocked his head to one side to gauge his impact on me. I tried to leave my face expressionless. He was not speaking idly, said Mr Pipinelis, Greece stood at the cross-roads. She would soon have a government of all the real talents and he believed I was one of these talents. I had not been called from abroad for nothing. If I followed the right course of action, as a member of 'their' loyal band, there would be no limits to how far I might rise. 'But we must now part, alas. We shall meet again soon. I have urgent work to complete. Remember: loyalty above all. It will take you far and you will be among your brothers in heart.' He did not rise. I bowed in greeting and left, seeing him still before my eyes as I was driven back to my office—Pipinelis, the diminutive grey eminence, lost in his grey wicker chair, in the grey room where we had met, a man in a grey suit who had taken me to the top of the mountain and shown me the kingdoms of the world.

What did I think of Pipinelis, the King asked me that afternoon. A most remarkable man, wasn't he? Pipinelis had the wisdom of Plato. I should be meeting him more often.

A succession of courtiers talked to me that day, all smiling knowingly and affectionately. They squeezed my hand, patted my shoulders and indicated with their gestures—rather than words—that they believed I had now truly joined them in spirit. They nearly all used the same words: 'You saw Mr Pipinelis. That's good. That's good."

It was time to get back to my work on Cyprus. Turkey was massing troops forty miles across the water from Cyprus. Turkish planes were flying over. There was fighting, started by who knows which frightened group. There were estimates of who killed how many. There was war in the air.

Tension between the palace and the Papandreous, father and son, grew daily for reasons that were not clear to me. The only thing clear was that the hostility had originated in the palace; George Papandreou, the Prime Minister, still strove to have good relations with the King. But the King did not seem to want a rapprochement. I wondered why?

My father provided the explanation: 'These names you gave me, of the officers who are visiting the palace, they are all part of a plot. There will be a coup. The leaders will be generals. The junior ones, Nasser Papadopoulos, Roufogalis, Ladas, Makarezos, Pattakos, are doing the dirty work. They will strike one night and overthrow the government.'

'How do you know, father?'

'There's been a coup in the air for a long time. It has always

90

been a sort of contingency plan. Now they are taking steps to make the plan a reality.'

'But how do you know, father, how can you be sure?'

'Shit boy,' said father, quite annoyed, 'who do you take me for? Intelligence work was my speciality for a long time. And I have been around a long time. There are Fascists I protected in the Middle East when they were suspect and the British would have put them in concentration camps. In Greece such debts are repaid, even by Fascists. One of them, Balopoulos—remember him, the fat young officer who always used to beat you at billiards—he told me the other day that he felt I had not been sufficiently honoured but that soon things would change and that he and people like him who valued heroism and patriotism would be in a position to honour me as befitted my services to Greece.'

'That's hardly proof, father.'

'Will you shut up and listen? I pretended I was very touched. I believe I even squeezed out a couple of tears and complained about Papandreou's shabby treatment of me. I could do that very convincingly because that old bastard Papandreou has treated me shabbily. Balopoulos said that I wouldn't have to wait long and that I would be given the honours due to me, anything I wanted, an ambassadorship to Paris. Then Balopoulos spoke of the corruption of the political world and of the need for the army to clean up the country. I was surprised when he gave me as an example the army revolution of 1909 which curbed the power of the King and did clean up politics, as a matter of fact. It was surprising to hear Balopoulos use that example; I always thought him a confirmed royalist.'

I told my father, then, about my conversation with Pipinelis and the tiny man's theories about a Platonic elite.

'So the hydrocephalous dwarf sees himself as the new Plato,' said father chuckling. 'At any rate, after my conversation with Balopoulos, I went to see my koumbaroi.'

A koumbaros is someone to whose child you have stood as god-father. The father of the child and the godfather are one another's koumbaros. My father was the godfather of countless children in Greece. He was sought after for the role because he was famous but also because he took the relationship seriously and used his influence on behalf of his koumbaroi and their off-spring or relatives.

'I have several koumbaroi even in the gendarmerie and in

KYP (KYP are the initials of the Greek CIA). Some are in fairly high positions, some are in lower positions. I visited them, to inspect my godchildren, taking a bottle, chocolates and some flowers along and they kept me to dinner. I got drunk and gave my anti-Papandreou speech. By the small hours, we were all drunk and many of them talked. The coup is no longer a contingency plan. It is a reality. Only the date has not been fixed.'

I still did not take my father's word for it but decided to check for myself. The first opportunity came at a US Embassy party. A US official introduced himself to me.[9]

'They call me a first secretary at the Embassy but I am with the CIA here. I have sixty full-time members of my staff which makes me more important than the ambassador, I guess, as anyone can see : my official car is bigger and more expensive than his,' he laughed. He was being very loud, surrounded by a group of men who obviously deferred to him.

'The situation must be worrying you, Sir,' I said. 'There seems to be a lot of tension in the air. Peace marches, anti-Vietnam demonstrations, anti-American articles in the press.'

'Not to mention that Communist Andreas Papandreou,' said an American colonel.

'Andreas,' said the CIA man, 'a real chameleon : a Trotskyist, then an American citizen who actually served in our Navy, and now he gives up American citizenship and becomes an anti-American.'

'A renegade,' said the colonel. 'Can you imagine someone giving up the privilege of being American?' To make his point clearer he switched to Greek which he spoke faultlessly. 'He is like Ephialtes who showed the Persians how to get behind Leonidas' 300 who were defending Thermopylae.'

'Surely you are going too far, colonel,' I said.

'I mean every word I say.'

'Which politician would you prefer,' I asked.

'I don't think much of politicians.'

'So there is no hope for us Greeks, then. We have no chance of being well-governed?'

'Not by your politicians, but there are other men.'

'Like whom,' I asked. 'I am new here; I have been away a very long time. I'd like to know the men on whom the country must rely to be well-governed.'

'Remember Colonel Papadopoulos, then,' said the American Colonel. 'He will govern you well.[10]

I moved away and went to talk to another US 'diplomat', I put his title in quotation marks because I have never quite been sure whether he was a true member of the American diplomatic service or of a more occult service. (It may be pure coincidence but shortly after this man was appointed to Italy—army plots began developing in that country.)

This 'diplomat' and I had known one another for many years. He speaks Greek fluently and knows Greece intimately. He gave me a long talk about the terrible impression that was being made on the US Congress by the fact that since the Liberals had come to power in 1963, some 'subversives' had been released from jail and that there now were anti-American demonstrations in Greece by students protesting against US involvement in the Vietnam war. He was also worried about a projected 'peace march' by students of various nationalities who had come to Greece. This sort of thing had not been happening before the Liberals came to power. He spoke bitterly about Andreas Papandreou: 'Can you imagine giving up US citizenship?'

The next day I had a long rambling discussion with Major Arnaoutis, the King's private secretary. I told him of my interest in Pericles, the great Athenian statesman, an honest and effective politician. 'If the truth were known,' Arnaoutis said, 'we should probably find out that Pericles had been as venal as all politicians. And didn't Pericles start the Peloponnesian war which destroyed Athens? And how about Alcibiades, Pericles' nephew and pupil, who betrayed Athens? Politicians were and always have been a disaster. The only way to save a country is to get rid of them.'

'Dictatorship?' I asked.

Arnaoutis laughed: 'Not dictatorship but a system in which all power rests in the hands of the King who appoints ministers and has the power to dismiss Parliament at any time.'

'What would Parliament do?'

'Vote the credits the King's ministers asked for,' said Arnaoutis.

Again I reported all these conversations to my father.

'I'm worried,' he said. 'I feel it in my bones. The coup is near. And the Americans here are backing it: all my sources say so.'

'Why would the Americans be against Prime Minister Papandreou? His politics, after all, correspond to those of the American Democratic party, father.'

'Skata. Old Papandreou engages in intellectual arguments with the Americans. He talks political philosophy at them. The

93

son, Andreas, is even worse : he has quoted the American declaration of independence to the Americans and he made it sound subversive.'

'Be serious father.'

'I am being serious, goddamit. To the Americans we are a base they have bought. They want no headaches, no lectures, no interviews to US journalists who then criticise the American government for not supporting democracy in the cradle of democracy. The Americans are businessmen. They have had a right wing caretaker in this property of theirs and were prepared to try a Liberal caretaker, but they will keep the Liberal only so long as he acts submissively like the old one.'

'You make us sound like a colony.'

'What did you think we were?'

I went to the beach. I asked Giorgos, my chauffeur-bodyguard if he cared to join me for lunch; fresh fish was being broiled on charcoal and my mouth was watering. Giorgos looked unhappy. I asked him what the matter was.

'I thought you were going to have your siesta at this time, Mr General and you aren't going to have a siesta.'

'You mean you wanted to have a siesta?' I knew he occasionally slept on the back seat.

'No, Mr General. I had hoped to visit my little nephew. He is crippled. He is in the hospital.'

'You can go if you want to.'

'I've missed the bus, Mr General. I could not go on the next bus. I would be away too long.'

'Take the car, then,' I said.

Giorgos stared at me speechless. When finally he spoke, he sounded unbelieving : 'Take your car? The Mercedes? To visit my nephew? Can I carry him down to show it to him?' (The car, incidentally, was my own property; I had brought it over from America : I would not use a palace car.)

Giorgos left after assuring me that he would never forget what he called 'this benefaction'. I asked the restaurant to set a table a little way along the beach, in the shade of a pine tree. There I was joined by an old acquaintance, the man who had refused to render me a service without a bribe.

'I have been trying to talk to you,' he said. 'It is difficult. You are being followed. I can't take much time. Your telephone is bugged. Your car is bugged. Your bed is bugged. Everything is bugged.'

'How do you know?' I asked.

'I know. Look at the head of your bed, in one of the legs. Also, the chandelier.'

He gave me all the locations. I asked how long the bugs had been in place.

'Only a few days. Only since you've been on the list, Mr General.'

'What list?'

'The list of those to be arrested on the day of the plan "Prometheus". I should not be saying this and don't repeat it. It is dangerous for me to tell you this. I must not be seen with you.'

'What of the man who is following me?'

'I am following you today, Mr General.' He strode away.

I watched him go, a big man, going to fat and losing some of his hair. He was perspiring freely and sweat had stained his flowered shirt.

I began watching eyes around me. I was stared at a lot in the palace. The stares were blank, especially those of the King and his Mother. I was still there, in my office, at the palace but I was cut off from them. Through Pipinelis they had made me an offer to join them and they sensed that I had turned it down. Now they had washed their hands of me. My obvious segregation from the other courtiers was accentuated by my increasing 'detachment'. As always, I reacted to a stressful situation as if it were something I was merely observing—not part of my life but a story that I was going to write.

I still wondered whether my imagination was running wild and so I looked for further information on what was afoot. I treated my perceptions with suspicion—I did not want to fool myself into believing something that was not.

What was I to make of the fact that American officials had begun calling Andreas Papandreou a Communist? The Papandreou cabinet was government of the political centre and the centre in Greece is sufficiently to the right to satisfy senator Barry Goldwater. Admittedly, the Papandreous—father and son—believed that more should be done in the field of welfare, that secondary education should be without charge, that the police existed to serve the citizens and not to rule them, but did this make Andreas Papandreou a 'Communist'?

Then, Greek Army officers began talking of what would happen, come the revolution—their revolution. Senior army officers, among them the chief of staff, made speeches deploring the 'degeneration of national morality'. These speeches were quoted by the US embassy information officers to visiting foreign correspondents.

At one of my meetings with Andreas Papandreou he showed me depositions from some officers who believed in the principle of civilian government, that the lines of all cabinet ministers were bugged on orders from Colonel George Papadopoulos, formerly of KYP (the Greek CIA). Papadopoulos had been transferred from KYP but the organisation still took its orders from him. After the fall of the colonels, Greek investigating judges gathered sworn testimony that George Papadopoulos received a personal stipend from the American CIA agents and that he was the man through whom they paid stipends to the rest of the KYP employees: to avoid confusion, I shall repeat one more time that the initials KYP in Greek stand for CIA in English, as in Central Intelligence Agency.

Andreas Papandreou gave the order for the wiretaps to be removed and for all such electronic surveillance to end. He was visited by Norbert Anshutz, the number two at the US Embassy who peremptorily ordered Andreas Papandreou, a Greek Cabinet Minister, to rescind the order abolishing the wiretaps. Andreas Papandreou asked Mr Anshutz to leave. The latter did leave, warning Papandreou that 'there would be consequences.'[11]

I decided to see the Prime Minister and tell him all the things I had heard. He received me at his modest little house in a suburb of Athens—the only property he owned after fifty years in political life and it was still mortgaged. George Papandreou was a very tall, almost theatrical man with an eloquence in ordinary speech which I could not possibly reproduce. I can only say that he was in a class with Demosthenes and Cicero and that, possibly, like them, he was, in a sense, the captive of his own brilliant eloquence.

I gave him my report and he listened courteously.

'I know that a coup is being prepared,' said the Prime Minister. 'I know all the names you gave me. Like your father, I have many koumbaroi who have warned me and there still are Greeks who believe that a democratically elected, majority government is worth preserving. My own Minister of War, Mr Petros Garoufalias protects the conspirators.[12] His membership in my Cabinet was imposed upon me by the palace, or rather, let us say that I accepted the King's suggestion that I appoint

Garoufalias to show that I had no intention of wresting control of the armed forces from the palace and its clique.'

'Why, then, if you haven't touched the armed forces, are they preparing a coup against you.'

'I can only surmise. The investigation of the assassination of Lambrakis is turning up evidence that is pointing straight to the palace. Then there are contracts that were given to American firms at terms outrageously unfavourable to Greece and there is strong evidence, documentary evidence, which points straight to the palace and its clique. Perhaps they are afraid that I shall bring out these things. I have proposed to keep it all quiet and to increase the Queen Mother's stipend. I suppose they consider this is monstrous insolence on my part that must be punished.'

'What will you do, Mr Prime Minister?'

'Defend myself. Fire Garoufalias as Defence Minister, if necessary. Replace the generals who are plotting the coup by others who are loyal royalists and therefore no threat to the King but who also believe that the army should stay out of politics. It all rests on whether I can convince the officer corps that my government does not represent a threat for them.'

A sinister figure from Greece's recent past emerged to counter the Prime Minister's campaign to gain the confidence of the army. General Grivas, the leader of the Cyprus insurrection, and a Fascist who had collaborated with the Germans in World War Two to track down and kill Greek resistance fighters, wrote a letter to King Constantine accusing Andreas Papandreou of having organised a secret army organisation to subvert the army. The name of this organisation, Grivas said, was ASPIDA, meaning shield.

It has been amply proved, since, that ASPIDA was no threat to the Greek armed forces.[13] Six captains who felt they had been denied merited promotions had banded together to petition for a redress of their grievance. In the Greek Army, as in other armies, any banding together is forbidden and punished with varying degrees of severity, depending on the purposes of those who banded together. So, the six captains who formed ASPIDA were guilty of conduct unbecoming to an officer. An inquiry was ordered and General Simos of the Army Advocate General's corps reached the conclusion, eventually, that there was no ASPIDA plot. (This general, incidentally, was subsequently thrown out of his post by the junta.)

The future junta seized on the ASPIDA revelation to create

an atmosphere of anxiety. A letter, allegedly by Prime Minister Papandreou, was published in an extremist rag. Later it was proven to be a forgery, but its appearance gave a semblance of truth to the slander that the Prime Minister himself was involved in an attempt to subvert the armed forces.

Andreas Papandreou, the Prime Minister's son, was accused of being the leader of ASPIDA. Testimony before the court trying the junta in August 1975 describes how the damaging rumours were manufactured, how witnesses were coached to lie and by whom. The names of those involved in this systematic campaign of calumny were put before the court.[14] George Papadopoulos was the leader of this operation. He has been found guilty.

George Papadopoulos was moved from Athens to a unit on the Turkish border. From this unit came a story of an attempt to sabotage the armed forces. Some rounds of rifle ammunition, three in all as subsequent investigations revealed, were found to have no charge. This happens not infrequently in all munition factory runs. Papadopoulos and his propaganda machine blew this up into a picture of Communist sabotage in the armed forces. Then Papadopoulos reported that the vehicles of his unit were being sabotaged. A private was arrested by Papadopoulos himself, beaten up and immersed into a cess-pool repeatedly until he 'confessed' that he had indeed sabotaged vehicles. The private's name is Matatis and he had the courage later to sue for defamation of character.[15]

There is evidence—and again the courts forbid the use of names until all judicial procedures have run their courses—connecting US psychological warfare experts with these activities. This evidence suggests that the Americans knew that the stories of subversion in the Greek army were false: some Americans, at least knew. And Americans certainly participated in the spreading of these wild accusations against the Liberal government;[16] many of them told me, to my face, that the Papandreou government was allowing the armed forces to be subverted, a fact denied since by a whole parade of right-wing, anti-Communist generals and distinguished civilians, among them Mr Panayotis Canellopoulos, former Prime Minister, the chiefs of the air force and the navy at the time of the coup, ministers in the present Conservative Greek government like Mr George Rallis, in short a who's-who of the Greek anti-Communist elite. That the colonels themselves, after they took power, never managed to produce evidence of such subversive activities, even though they tortured the members of ASPIDA was irrelevant; the base-lessness of the charges would be demonstrated too late.

The US military mission in Greece began speaking of the ASPIDA 'plot' as if it were a reality and a plan for the Communist subversion of the Greek armed forces. The complicity of Andreas Papandreou was taken for granted. He resigned his cabinet portfolio so that it could not be said that he would use his ministerial powers to shield himself.

The right wing press generated an atmosphere of hysteria. The senior officers who were in on the coup preparations—they held the top posts in the army—began a campaign of 'vigilance', as they called it, to warn the officer corps against the 'planned' ASPIDA coup. The plan PROMETHEUS was practised several times: this was a NATO plan designed to prevent a Communist takeover of a NATO country.

The situation was Kafkaesque in its improbability: a small nucleus of army officers who had plotted for years to take power were approaching their goal, even though the aims of this group had been known for years and efforts had been made by both Conservative and Liberal governments to neutralise the group.

As far back as 1956, the activities of the plotters had been discovered by an officer of the 2nd Bureau (Intelligence) of the Greek General Staff. This officer, Mr Zacharopoulos, now a Brigadier General, photographed the plotters and taped their comments.[17] Later, on orders of the current Prime Minister, Mr Caramanlis, the then chief of the Army Staff, General Nicolopoulos, tried to cashier the plotters who were continuing their activities but the plotters had strong protectors and it was General Nicolopoulos who was thrown out of the Army.

In 1964, they were again discovered to be plotting and the Papandreou government transferred most of them from their posts in Athens to provincial commands. Mr Michael Papaconstantinou, then under-secretary of defence was called to the palace and asked by the King: 'Are you trying to destroy the armed forces?'

A council of lieutenant generals, all of them royalists, decided in 1964 that Gregory Spandidakis, one of the plotters, was not worthy of promotion and had to be retired. During the meeting, a phone call to the Minister of Defence saved Spandidakis. There is no clear evidence whether the phone call was from the palace or from the Americans.[18] I know of my own knowledge that Major Arnaoutis, the King's private secretary, was saying at the time that those who sought to retire Spandidakis would not be allowed to get away with it. A member of the US Embassy also expressed his indignation to me at what he called attempts to victimise Spandidakis. The fact is Spandidakis' military superiors had found him lacking in the qualities justifying promotion. There was no political motive behind the attempt by the army hierarchy to retire him. But he was a member of the charmed group of plotters who had such strong protectors.

Meanwhile I had found the microphones in my bed, in the chandelier and in my car. I left them there, of course. Had I taken them out, new microphones would have been placed in new locations. The right wing press began calling me a 'Socialist' who had come to Greece to help British Socialists by selling Greece out on Cyprus. The left wing press began accusing me of being a monarcho fascist who had come to Greece to help the British Conservatives by selling Greece out on the Cyprus issue.

No proof was advanced : journals of the extreme left and the extreme right do not allow such things as facts to interfere with their writing. Apparently, little proof was needed. The accusations were at least partially believed.

'So your friend Andreas Papandreou is heading a secret society in the armed forces,' said the King. He had just come back from playing squash with his favourite partner, an American lieutenant colonel who was working for the CIA.

I told the King I did not believe Andreas Papandreou was involved in any army plot. 'Look who is accusing him, Your Majesty. You can't believe such rags.'

The King was towelling his head. He had obviously had a good, hard game and was glowing with health. 'Those rags, as you call them,' he said, 'attribute their stories to "unimpeachable and highly placed sources".'

'When the left wing rags slander the Royal family, Your Majesty, they also quote "unimpeachable and highly placed sources".'

'That's different. Communist papers do not have access to unimpeachable, highly placed sources. Nationalist papers have such access.'

'But who are those sources, Your Majesty?'

'They might be army officers. They would be unimpeachable sources, would they not?'

My father warned me that people were talking about me too. 'They say that since no denial was issued, there must be something to the stories about you. People say there never is smoke without fire. And then, you have written articles saying that George Blake was not a Communist spy.'

Blake, a member of British Intelligence, had been in prison with me, in North Korea. We had become friends. When he was arrested and tried for treason, in the 1960's I found it very hard to believe that he could have been converted to Communism in prison camp—as the prosecution alleged. Blake was an intelligent and compassionate man. Could he have been converted to a doctrine in whose name old missionaries were allowed to die of extreme privation and ill-treatment in North Korean camps? Could he have been converted to a doctrine in whose name we had been beaten with rifle butts—he and I—while being made to kneel in the snow, in summer clothes with temperatures well below zero?

'Nevertheless,' said my father, 'people do ask why these calumnies have not been denied.'

'But what am I to deny? Should I say that I am not, have not been and will never be a Communist, Socialist or Monarchofascist; that I never have nor ever will sell the Greek Cypriots down the river? Let me give you the answer these rags will print : "Technically, the denial may be correct in the sense that Gigantes is not a card carrying Communist and in the sense that he has not received payment for selling out the Greek Cypriots. But a denial was to be expected. Can Gigantes *prove* that he is not a Communist? Can he prove that he is not plotting against the Greek Cypriots?" That's what they'll answer, father.'

And the next thing that happened was that people began asking why I was not suing the papers which had slandered me. Others had sued and the punishment meted out by the courts did not prevent further calumnies. All around me, the words 'there is no smoke without fire' became more audible by the day.

'We're going to have to put some interesting items in your dossier in Washington,' said the man with the ultra-large limousine who advertised himself as the CIA chief in Greece.

'Be a good lad,' I answered, 'go play 007 somewhere else.' My dominant feeling was still one of unreality. It was as if I had tried to think up the more extreme and least likely consequences of my being Secretary General to the King of Greece, and by the very fact that I had thought them out, they had acquired a perverse reality of their own.

I went to see the US 'diplomat' I had known for many years.

'It's very confusing,' I said. 'Your embassy is calling the Papandreou government leftist. Your military attaches are calling Andreas Papandreou a Communist. Why? The current government in Greece is the closest, ideologically, to your Democratic Party. It's a pro-western, pro-American government. Why are you people doing all this?'

'We were thinking of inviting you to dinner,' my US acquaintance said, 'but it has not been possible. You must be awfully busy with arrangements for the King's wedding.'

'You haven't answered me. Why are you people doing all this?'

'I don't know what you're talking about.'

I tried a little longer—unsuccessfully—then left.

Was I imagining things? Were the US military attaches talking out of turn? Was the man who called himself the chief of the CIA, a mere clown? He had asked me at a dinner party what I thought we should do about a peace march that an international group of long haired youngsters had planned:

'You gotta break it up with clubs and water cannon and police dogs. A leftist government is already suspect. If this march takes place and you do not break it up, Congress will cut all aid to Greece.'

Such threats had been used before. In 1950, the American embassy in Athens made such threats, in writing, to force the resignation of a Greek government it did not like. That was the famous Grady letter, named after ambassador Henry F. Grady who signed it. The next American Ambassador, Peurifoy, overthrew a couple of Greek governments before going to Guatemala to organise the coup that toppled President Arbenz in 1954.

I tried counter-threatening: 'I have friends in high places in Washington. How would you like them to hear that you try to push a Greek official like me around?' I asked.

The CIA man grinned broadly: 'Tell them, sonny. Go ahead and tell them. That'll get me a promotion and it will probably teach you on which side your bread is buttered. Because if you try to cross us, we'll break you. It's really easy. I'll begin giving you some proof of how easy it is to break you.'

That very week a right wing member of the Greek Parliament with CIA connections began telling people that I had collaborated with the Communists when I had been a prisoner of war in Korea and that I had made pro-Communist broadcasts. He claimed to have tapes of such broadcasts.[19]

He must have been very busy telling this story because a succession of acquaintances sought me out to ask whether this was true. I always answered that it was not and that they should ask to hear the tapes of my alleged broadcasts. My acquaintances would invariably say that my answer was good but there was doubt left in their eyes.

Two weeks later, I met the CIA man again : 'How do you like having a reputation, Phil?' he asked smiling broadly. 'Would you like to have a crust of bread and some butter with me?'

By that time, my work on how to present the Greek case on Cyprus had progressed sufficiently for the Prime Minister to start thinking of whom to entrust with this mission. He offered me the job and I accepted.

'I was wondering how long you would stay at the palace,' said George Papandreou. He was standing in the library of his house some miles out of Athens. Now that I think of it, he seems to have been standing every time we met, exuding an aura of vigour. The Prime Minister was in his late seventies or early eighties—he was not very forthcoming about his age. He was extremely vigorous and seemed to have the energy of a man half his age, as many fashionable ladies were anxious to assert.

'Do you remember our first meeting, ever, before you left for Korea where you were made prisoner, in 1950?' he asked.

It had not been a forgettable meeting. The American ambassador, Henry F. Grady, had written his letter to the Greek government asking it to choose between either resigning or losing US aid. George Papandreou had opposed that particular Greek government; my father had supported it. I had published a summary of the Grady letter and the government had fallen. On the day that government had fallen, George Papandreou had seen me at the entrance of the Greek parliament buildings and had thrown open his arms shouting: 'Let me embrace you. You are the architect of my new government.'

I was clasped to his bosom and I remember feeling rather silly, if only because of the setting—the tall doric columns, the marble steps, the kilted guards, the tourists with their cameras, probably taking our picture, and Papandreou's retinue of petitioners who fastened on to me as soon as he stepped into his car to be driven away. Would I use my obvious influence with Papandreou, the petitioners asked? Would I help their sons, daughters, sisters, brothers, with jobs, pensions, promotions? Would I tell Papandreou to tell the university to let some son graduate even though he failed the exams: 'He is such a good boy and he works at two jobs to look after his mother and sisters. He could not study. He deserves to graduate.'

Now that I was joining him, said the Prime Minister, he wanted to show me documentary evidence that what he had told me and what I had surmised was true. I would need to know such things of my own knowledge. But the Prime Minister wanted my promise that I would tell no one of what I would see shortly.

'Tell no one, ever, under any circumstances, Mr Prime Minister?'

He was not asking for eternal silence, he said. I would see that I should not say these things for some time—if I spoke, Papandreou's efforts to affect a reconciliation between his party and the monarchy would fail. When that issue no longer mattered, I might speak if I thought it appropriate.

He let me read four dossiers which contained documentary evidence that proved four grave accusations: one, that with the approval of the palace, the current military leadership falsified the results of the 1961 election; two, that the military leadership, with the blessing of the palace, was preparing a coup against Papandreou and was using the menace of such a coup to make Papandreou bow to their will; three, that the gendarmerie and the army were involved in the murder of Gregory Lambrakis, the left wing deputy, and in this case too there was complete documentary evidence leading to the palace; four, that a huge contract was awarded to a US firm before Papandreou came to power in 1963; it could not be more disadvantageous to Greece and in this case too there was clear documentary evidence which pointed to a bribe of one million dollars given to 'one of the highest personage in the land'.

The evidence consisted of photographed documents which were truly damning.

Prime Minister George Papandreou, who had left the room, walked in on me as I was finishing my examination of the fourth dossier. He wanted to know what I thought.

Was the evidence unassailable, I asked. If those documents were fabrications, they would sound true; fabrications are often more authentic than the real thing. Besides, it seemed to me incredible that the government Papandreou had replaced had not destroyed the evidence. The evidence on electoral fraud implicated a lot of people in criminal acts.

Evidence was difficult to destroy completely, in these days of photography, said the Prime Minister. Those inculpated by the papers I had seen, had put their trust in the wrong people who were betraying now. The hewers of wood and carriers of water, the small people involved in all the dirty business, were afraid. They had lost their political protectors. They had no guarantee they would not be prosecuted. So they were turning state's evidence, the Prime Minister said.

The coup that was being prepared, the Prime Minister said, had as its aim to keep him from using this evidence, keep him from prosecuting those who were involved in stealing the 1961 elections; keep him from pressing on with the investigation of Lambrakis' murder; keep him from renegotiating the contract with that American firm. As far as we knew, no one in the army was involved in the contract negotiations; no one in the army stood to lose anything if the government investigated the circumstances under which the contract was awarded. Why, then, was the army warning off Papandreou? Whom was the army protecting? Who, in other words, was the 'one of the highest personage in the land' mentioned in the dossier?

Was he going to use the evidence, I asked.

He could not be Prime Minister, Papandreou said and have, at the head of the armed forces, people who falsified a general election in 1961. He could not be Prime Minister and leave, at the head of the gendarmerie, people who plotted the murder of a member of Parliament. He could not be Prime Minister, Papandreou said, and let those guilty officers threaten him with a coup d'etat. He could not let an American company rob Greece, simply because that company bribed the right people.

They would overthrow him, I said. He was threatening the armed forces. They had built a political army, over the years. They would not let him change it. The Royal Family believed it could hold on to the throne only if it were sure of the army. The Americans, too, had a stake in the army as it was constituted.

He would not take the army away from the palace or from the Americans, said George Papandreou. He would not try to give army commands to officers who might claim they were Liberals. He would leave things in the hands of royalist officers, but royalist officers who had shown respect for the constitution and the laws—there were such officers, the Prime Minister said. Above all, he would not pursue the leads which seemed to incriminate the palace; maybe the Royal Family would trust him and other Liberals if he protected the palace.

'On ne pardonne jamais un bienfait—they might never forgive you for protecting them, Mr Prime Minister.'

Maybe not, he said. He was gambling. He needed time in which to prove to both the palace and the Americans that they had nothing to fear from him and the political centre. He might lose the gamble.

Before leaving for Washington, I knew I had to face Queen Frederika the Queen Mother. I have earlier spoken of her charm and obvious love for her late husband, her energy and her indefatigable work on behalf of wounded soldiers. These were her attractive traits. However, she had other traits that can only be described as menacing. She had hounded her husband's first cousin, Prince Peter of Greece, whose support for strictly constitutional forms of monarchy went counter to her views of monarchs who not only reign but rule by divine right. She had Prince Peter struck from the rolls of the Greek army despite his distinguished wartime service in World War Two. She had publicly called him a Communist and even written this accusation to the late King of Denmark. Prince Peter of Greece has documentary proof of all these acts and has made them public. She intervened to keep him from teaching anthropology at the University of Athens, even though he had all the formal qualifications for such a post and is an eminent anthropologist.

She demanded and obtained the trial and conviction on a charge of lèse-majesté of an Athens editor who had published the undisputed fact that Queen Frederika's brothers had served as German SS officers in Greece during World War Two.

She had fancied herself insulted by Gregory Lambrakis, the Greek member of Parliament. The 'insult' was his request to the Queen's equerry for an audience in which Lambrakis wanted to plead for the release of an imprisoned Communist. Like Henry the Second of England, Queen Frederika had exclaimed: Won't someone rid me of this man? Senior police officers arranged the murder of Lambrakis through a royalist terrorist organisation. Mr Constantine Kollias, one of the Queen Mother's creatures and chief prosecutor of the Greek Supreme Court, had done his best to suppress any investigation of the murder of Lambrakis. (The Palace, later, as we shall see, rewarded Mr Kollias by making him Prime Minister.)

By the time I was to see Queen Frederika, prior to my

departure for Washington, I knew all about the murder of Lambrakis. As I have written, George Papandreou had shown me documents implicating persons very close to the Palace. It should be noted, also, that several witnesses in the Lambrakis case died in a surprising succession of accidents. To have knowledge of what happened to Lambrakis was to be in danger of becoming a victim of an unexplained accident, such as 'committing suicide by jumping from the secret police headquarters.'

Then there were the Queen Mother's conversations with the hereafter. She told me once that her dead husband was in paradise and came to see her to tell her what the will of God was with regards to Greece. She had asked me to publicise the fact. I had had great difficulty in convincing her that we should keep the matter quiet because 'people would not understand'.

Should the last paragraph appear too fantastic, I would like to quote Prince Peter of Greece in an interview he gave to the Greek newspaper *TA NEA*:

'On the day of the memorial service at Tatoi (the summer palace) for the late King Paul, and before we entered the church, Frederika said to Constantine (the young King): "but why do we have to have a memorial service? Paul came in the night and told me, he was in Paradise. That I (Frederika) will now govern my land. Let's go celebrate the event in the fields." Constantine answered: "Mother, we have to have a memorial service because we brought the people over." Ten minutes after the beginning of the memorial service, Frederika left the church and later said she had met the late King Paul outside his grave and that he had said, "tell Constantine to do as you say. That is my paternal and royal advice." And then (this is still a direct quotation from Prince Peter), my cousin Michael who was there asked me in French "do you believe she is quite well in her health?" '

So it was with some considerable ambivalence that I walked in to see Queen Frederika. I had prepared myself by obtaining a medical certificate which said that further stay in Greece was bad for the health of my daughter for whom the move from Washington to Athens had meant the simultaneous loss of her house, her friends, her home-town, her mother tongue and all that was familiar and safe in her life: that the articles in the press attacking me as a Communist (and obligingly translated to her by neighbours) had caused her great anxiety and that this had given her a severe case of nervous asthma. All of which was true.

But the Queen dismissed all this. She was fuming, and she fumed for a good long while during which she accused me of having used her son to climb to my new rank of Minister of Culture going to Washington with Ambassadorial rank and that I was doing this because I had had the insolent presumption to doubt her judgment and trust my own about statecraft in which her family had been occupied for centuries. The variations on these two themes lasted so long that I lost my manners and retorted that her family had not done so well in statecraft considering the constant diminution of its domains in Europe over the centuries.

I apologised for my tone but, surprisingly, she was not offended.

'I like your outbursts,' she said, smiling. Then her smile changed and she added, 'but I'll never forgive you for leaving my son to join his enemies': the King's enemies, presumably being his legally and democratically elected ministers.

The policeman who had revealed to me the location of the electronic devices spying on me, came to see me that night. 'I have my annual leave, Mr General,' he said. 'With your permission, I shall watch over you discreetly until you leave. I am a good shot. I won't let them get you.'

By then, I was living in a house lent to me by my old school, a teacher's residence, empty for the summer. My volunteer protector had rapped on the kitchen window in the dead of night. I had opened the window, he had spoken and vanished.

He was not my only protector. I had told my father of the scene with Queen Frederika and several of father's koumbaroi, all of them good shots, according to him, were also keeping discreet watch over me. Several times, a restraining hand kept me from crossing a street as a motor car shaved the sidewalk. Father also saw to it that a steady publicity was kept up in the Liberal press about my mission to Washington and the expected results.

'Publicity is protection under the circumstances,' father said.

And so, I got back to Washington in the early summer of 1964 to plead the Greek case on Cyprus and to plead for the right of Greece to stay democratic. I was going to be a very small antagonist for Lyndon Johnson, should he decide to turn against Greece, either on Cyprus or on whether Greece could remain a constitutional democracy and not become one more military dictatorship among American satellites.

108

I met with Robert Kennedy. He was no longer wielding·
power—his brother was dead but he was feared by Lyndon
Johnson. Robert Kennedy had grown marvellously, I thought,
grown through the responsibility that had been given to him by
his brother, the late President. He had been over-aggressive and
sometimes strident. But the cares of office and his brother's death
had mellowed him. At a young age, he was showing the stigmata
of the statesman. We met by pre-arrangement at the house of a
mutual friend, Marguerite Higgins, the late, great journalist.
We were left alone and I made my case for democracy in Greece.
The Papandreou government, I said, was a moderate, pro-
western government and it was being badly pressured by the
right, and the US embassy in Athens seemed to be taking sides
against the Papandreou government.

Robert Kennedy did not answer at once. He had developed
the capacity for reflection before speaking. 'I know,' he said
eventually. 'I know that our people are turning against
Papandreou.'

'Can't someone in Washington stop them?' I asked.

'Maybe. But someone would have to believe that our people
in Greece are wrong.'

'They are wrong.'

'You think so,' he said. 'But our files in the CIA, the Pentagon
and the State Department do not say so. Those files say that
Papandreou and his men—and I guess that includes you—are
not reliable.'

'Why are we not reliable?'

'Not reliable allies, I guess,' he said.

'Do you believe that?'

'Maybe not—not entirely, at least. But then I have had time
to get to know the quality of some reports we receive from
abroad. These reports are no better than the men who write
them and I know some of those men.'

'You are implying—you are almost saying—that the reports
from Greece which claim Papandreou is unreliable are false.'

'Not exactly,' said Robert Kennedy. 'I implied I knew the
people who wrote the reports, in the sense that I know some of
their biases. They've made a career of Greece. They started there
after World War Two, helped the Greeks defeat the Communist
guerrillas. Now these same Americans—some of them at least—
are in Greece writing reports. They still seem to see Greece from
the perspective of the fight against the Communists. They still

109

see Greece as two camps, the pro-Communists and the anti-Communists.'

'But surely that's wrong.'

'You tell me it's wrong,' said Robert Kennedy, 'but the weight of the evidence in our files—files accumulated over the past twenty years—tells me, or anybody else who reads the files, that there are two types of Greeks, those of the right wing with whom we have worked and on whom we can rely and the rest on whom we would be taking a chance. What I am telling you is that if you want the Americans in Greece to stop favouring your right wing, you have your work cut out. You'll have to convince Lyndon that you, a foreigner, are right and that a great number of Americans are wrong. You better get yourself some American to speak for you, someone Lyndon trusts in foreign affairs.'

'Whom are you suggesting?' I asked.

'Someone like Dean Acheson. He admires Lyndon and Lyndon is delighted to be admired by someone as patrician as Acheson.'[20] Robert Kennedy drifted away, to circulate among the other guests, asking questions, listening attentively with the hurt look that had not left his eyes since his brother's death. This was the time he was thinking of his future—what would he do since Lyndon would never offer him the vice-presidency? This was a question which empassioned everyone at Marguerite Higgins' party. To them all, Robert Kennedy was marked for greatness, even though he looked so weary.

Kennedy had given me a lot of time, more time than he had given me since I had come back from seeing Castro take Cuba. He had taken me aside then, at Marguerite Higgins' house again, and had wanted to know all about Cuba. I had told him that whatever might happen, Cubans would not support a US move against Castro: Cubans preferred Castro to the Yankees. After the Bay of Pigs, Robert Kennedy remembered I had disagreed with the information his brother had been receiving on Cuba. This had served as a basis for a fair acquaintanceship.

So I set out to hire Dean Acheson for Greece. He was practising law, one of the senior partners of Covington and Burling. Would a former secretary of state agree to act for a foreign country? Acting for foreign countries, of course, was a commonplace for the great American law firms but I was not sure Acheson would accept. In any case, his firm agreed to represent Greece in dealings with the US government. Other lawyers would do the day to day work—the work on maritime treaties, trade pacts. Mr Acheson would be available for the crucial issues, like Cyprus or the bias of US diplomats and military men in favour of the opponents of democracy in Greece.

I was glad to have Acheson's help with Lyndon Johnson, and not only because the US President was much more likely to listen to a former secretary of state but also because in the presence of Lyndon Johnson I felt embarrassment at best and, at worst, revulsion. Admittedly, such feelings were a reflection of my own prejudices against a certain type of man.

I had watched him operate for years: he had star billing in Washington. And he had granted me an interview when I worked as a newspaperman in Washington. The interview scared me. It seemed to go on for hours. He took me around with him, showing me his power and his domain. He stood in an entrance of the US Senate and worked to get Senator Everett Dirksen's vote. As he spoke, Lyndon Johnson pushed Dirksen against the wall and massaged him—literally. The treatment obviously worked: Dirksen voted the way Lyndon wanted.

'I like to press the flesh,' said Lyndon Johnson to me, pressing me against a wall and talking from so close that I felt he might bite my nose. The letters 'LBJ' shone in gold all around, from his cuff links, his tie clasp, a badge in his lapel. They were embroidered on his shirt. I began seeing those initials everywhere.

He took me back to one of his immense offices and summoned a secretary, a spectacular blonde.

'Watch how she jiggles as she struts,' said Lyndon Johnson. 'You don't see such high spirited strutting nor jiggling every day.' When she had traversed the quarter acre of carpet, he instructed her to retrace her steps and—loud enough for her to hear—he said, 'now watch the back view and refresh yourself before we get down to business.'

The interview itself had been depressing. At that stage in his career, in the late nineteen fifties, Lyndon Johnson had a comic strip vision of the world, with American supermen fighting Communist evil everywhere, while lesser nations, like Greece, expressed their gratitude for US generosity. He assured me that we, in the rest of the world, had a lot to be thankful for, considering that America was taking an interest in our affairs.

My next meeting face to face with him was on the evening of President Kennedy's burial. I was working for the United Nations at the time and had accompanied U Thant, the Secretary General, to the reception Lyndon Johnson was giving in the State Department. Many heads of state wished to speak with the new American president and he would take them aside to a corner of the vast reception room where a small sofa and three armchairs had been grouped.

The Secretary General of the United Nations rated a private conference. I accompanied him, and Lyndon Johnson summoned Adlai Stevenson who was at the reception. Quite unexpectedly, Stevenson began giggling: 'Tell them, Lyndon,' he said, 'tell them that I just missed being where you now are, President of the US. Tell them, tell them.'[21]

Stevenson went on giggling and in a heavy aside Lyndon Johnson said to the Secretary General of the United Nations, 'Pay no mind to Adlai, Mr Secretary General. Pay no mind to him at all. He sits down to piss and, naturally, he has nerves.' Obviously, Lyndon Johnson found this remark very funny for he burst out laughing, drawing a shocked look from General de Gaulle who was standing nearby.

Dean Acheson, the patrician, often expressed admiration for Lyndon Johnson. In the late nineteen fifties, Acheson had advised Johnson, when the latter was trying to establish a reputation as a statesman, in preparation for contesting the presidential nomination of the Democratic party in the 1960 elections. Having Acheson on our side made us feel a little better. In any case, the US was immersed in its presidential campaign in the summer of 1964 and was less interested than usual in foreign affairs. Johnson wanted to project an image of wisdom and flexibility, to contrast himself with his opponent, Senator Goldwater. The image of wisdom and flexibility encompassed all fields. Crisis abroad did not fit this image.

Lyndon Johnson invited the Prime Ministers of Greece and Turkey to Washington. In a brief private meeting with Prime Minister Papandreou, he talked of partitioning Cyprus.

Papandreou said that even if he agreed with partition, he could never get the Greek Parliament to accept partition.

That was unfortunate, said Johnson, because if Greece did not agree with partition, then the United States would have to rethink the aid it was giving Greece within the framework of NATO.

'All right,' said Papandreou, 'and in that case, Greece might have to rethink the advisability of belonging to NATO.'

'Maybe Greece should rethink the advisability of a Parliament which could not take the right decision,' Lyndon Johnson replied.

Papandreou was weary after the meeting. The Greek Ambassador to Washington, Alecos Matsas, congratulated Papandreou on refusing to be threatened—the Prime Minister had recounted his conversation with Johnson.[22]

'I regret that,' said the Greek Prime Minister. 'I regret speaking as I did. We are small. We can't talk as if we were big. I can't afford pride and yet I let my pride guide my thought.' He left for Greece with the feeling that his days in power were numbered.

In Greece, Andreas Papandreou was put under considerable pressure by embassy and CIA men, to repair the bad impression his father had made on Lyndon Johnson: these men urged Andreas to state that, in effect, the most important thing for Greece was devotion to NATO. He replied that he believed in Greece's right to take an independent line in foreign policy while still remaining a NATO member—something like Denmark. The words 'dangerous leftist' became a stereotype description of Andreas Papandreou.

In Washington, meanwhile, Dean Acheson was appointed by Lyndon Johnson as mediator in the Cyprus dispute. Acheson produced a plan which went counter to the instructions he had received as the lawyer for Greece. His plan said that:
—Cyprus would become Greek.
—There would be self-governing Turkish cantons.
—There would be a Turkish military base on Cyprus with no limit on the amount of troops and material to be stationed in that base.
—Greece would give Turkey—as the price of peace—the Greek island of Castelorizo.[23]

Alecos Matsas, the Greek Ambassador, was called by the White House. Lyndon Johnson listed the conditions of Acheson's plan.

'As Prime Minister Papandreou told you,' said Ambassador Matsas, 'no Greek Parliament could accept such a plan. At any rate, the Greek constitution does not allow a Greek government to give away a Greek island.'

'Then listen to me, Mr Ambassador,' said Lyndon Johnson, 'fuck your Parliament and your Constitution. America is an elephant. Cyprus is a flea. Greece is a flea. If those two fleas continue itching the elephant, they may just get whacked by the elephant's trunk, whacked good.'

'I shall communicate your views to the Prime Minister,' said Ambassador Matsas. 'But I have already told you what the Prime Minister's answer will be: Greece is a democracy; the Prime Minister cannot act against the wishes of Parliament.'

'Let me tell you what answer I will give if I get that sort of reply back from your Prime Minister,' said Lyndon Johnson. 'Who does he take himself for, anyway? I can't have a second de Gaulle on my hands. We pay a lot of good American dollars to the Greeks, Mr Ambassador. If your Prime Minister gives me talk about Democracy, Parliament and Constitutions, he, his Parliament and his Constitution may not last very long.'

'I must protest your manner, Mr President,' said Alecos Matsas. 'As the representative of Greece, an ally of your country, I cannot accept such treatment.' Lyndon Johnson shouted: 'Don't forget to tell old Papa what's his name what I told you. Mind you tell him. You hear?'

The Ambassador was trembling with humiliation. He asked me into his office and told me what had happened. I congratulated him on his stand. He shook his head hopelessly: 'They'll overthrow the government. I am a royalist. I want the young King to be a rallying point for the Greek nation. I am mortally afraid that he will be badly advised by the Americans now and that he will act unconstitutionally, endangering the throne.'

Mr Matsas wrote his report giving a full accounting of what President Johnson had said;[24] a fastidious man, Alecos Matsas found it repugnant to record the coarse words the US president had used. Finally the report was done, with every last vulgarity. The Ambassador gave it to the coding clerk who started sending on the radio teleprinter we had purchased from the Americans. This is a machine that automatically codes a message. The machine is supposed to have the capacity to vary its codes infinitely so that deciphering should be impossible.

Within minutes after the message was sent, Ambassador Matsas received a telephone call from Lyndon Johnson:

'Are you trying to get yourself in my bad books, Mister Ambassador?' asked Johnson. 'Do you want me to get really angry with you? That was a private conversation me and you had. You had no call putting in all them words I used on you. Watch your step.' And the President of the United States hung up.

'Do you think,' Ambassador Matsas asked me, 'that the Americans have sold us a tricked coding machine?'

Thereafter, when we had messages we wanted to keep super secret, we did not send them on the machine; we did not write them down: we flew to Athens and told the Prime Minister what he needed to know.

Turkish invasion threats increased. Cyprus said she would ask for weapons from Russia and Egypt. Cyprus' threat was enough to highly alarm the Americans. They demanded that Papandreou condemn this Cypriot initiative. The Papandreous said they would condemn any talk of an arms deal between Cyprus and Russia, provided the Americans guaranteed that Turkey would not be allowed to invade Cyprus. Lyndon Johnson was angered and Ambassador Matsas had to submit to more presidential abuse.

This American attitude brought to the surface a sentiment that had been growing in Greece for some time; the sentiment that the Americans exacted too high a price for whatever protection they gave to Greece. Greece, as a member of NATO, maintained an enormous military establishment, the largest per capita armed force of any NATO country. Only a small part of the military cost was borne by the US, the rest of the burden kept the Greek economy from soaring. This military establishment was not armed to defend Greece against any probable or even possible enemy—it was no match for the forces of Turkey or Bulgaria, let alone those of Russia. The Greek armed forces served mainly as the prop of a certain social and political pattern of life, a right wing pattern that preached blind allegiance to the US and did business with Americans on terms that profited the average Greek less than was right. All these sentiments came to the fore because of what the Greeks saw as American partiality towards Turkey.

There were reasons for that partiality: Turkish bases, close to Russia's borders, provided the US with valued sites for electronic observation of Russian military movements. Then, Turkey controlled the Bosphorus and the Dardanelles, the narrow straits through which all Russian shipping towards the Mediterranean had to pass. To maintain good relations with Turkey, the Americans were prepared to submit to indignities—such as the beating and homosexual rape of their servicemen stationed in Turkey. Turkish negotiations with Russia did not cause Washington to threaten the Turks, with one exception that coincided with the 1964 presidential elections in the United States. Lyndon Johnson wanted to win by the biggest landslide in history. He also wanted to show that he had strong 'coat-tails', i.e. that his own vote-getting powers would carry along to resounding victory Democratic candidates to federal and state offices.

The crisis in Cyprus was a threat to Johnson's hopes of triumph because US citizens of Greek descent mobilised as never before to demand that the US prevent the threatened Turkish invasion of Cyprus: if the invasion took place, the Greek Americans said they would vote Republican. So a stiff US note was sent to the Turks, threatening a cut-off in all forms of American aid if the invasion took place.

Lyndon Johnson won his massive victory and things went back to normal: smaller and less important to US military and intelligence needs than Turkey, Greece was run with a much heavier hand by Washington.

At any rate, in the last half of 1964 and the first six months of 1965, an obvious majority of the Greek people expressed their dislike of the particular relationship that existed between their country and the US. They wanted to remain the allies of the US, to remain within NATO, but they wanted the sort of independence that other allies of the US showed; the Greeks wanted to be as free as the Danes and the Norwegians are within NATO. Andreas Papandreou became the voice of this movement in Greece. He said that it was in the interest not only of the Greeks but of the Americans also to have the relations between the two countries change so that Greece would be less of a satellite and more of a free and willing ally.

He also spoke of economic reform, of foreign investments that would suit the real needs of Greece, leading to the development of its economy—not investments which gave the foreign investors privileges and profits that prevailed elsewhere only in colonial situations.

Andreas Papandreou also spoke of the wasteful* and unnecessary burden of armed forces too large for the economy and equipped only for internal repression.

Popular reaction to his speeches became more and more enthusiastic. Opinion polls showed that his popularity was rising. The Americans in Greece saw Andreas Papandreou as a threat to their position. Further, they saw him as a traitor.

Marguerite Higgins reported to me a conversation she had had with Lyndon Johnson who had said that Papandreou had 'betrayed America'. When she asked for an explanation, Johnson said: 'We gave the son of a bitch American citizenship, didn't we? He was an American, with all the rights and privileges. And he had sworn allegiance to the flag. And then he gave up his American citizenship. He went back to just being a Greek. You can't trust a man who breaks his oath of allegiance to the flag of these United States.'

Marguerite Higgins was intrigued by this story. Like the great journalist she was, she looked at all its aspects. We had been friends ever since the Korean war, where we had both served at the front as correspondents. She came to ask me about the views of Andreas Papandreou. I gave her some of Andreas' speeches to read.

She came to see me again. 'Your friend doesn't sound Communistic to me,' she said, 'but our people in Greece say he is a Communist.'

'The right wing press calls him a Communist, Marguerite. They called me a Communist.'

'It's not the Greek press that our sources quote but some of their best intelligence contacts.'

'What's a best intelligence contact?' I asked. 'A stool pigeon who sells information to both sides, a person who tells you what you want to hear? Remember your best intelligence contacts at the time of the Bay of Pigs? How accurate were they in their predictions of Castro's collapse.'

'These people are not stool pigeons,' said Marguerite Higgins. 'They are Greek intelligence officers whom we have trained and we have taught them all we know. I'm told they are very good, very professional.' She stopped talking and looked at me a good long while then she said: 'I've always trusted you; you know that. I am interested in this story and so I want to use all you know. I am going to tell you something but only if you swear you will not use it.'

'I can't swear that, Marguerite. I work for the Greek Government. I represent it here in Washington as does Ambassador Matsas. If you tell me something the Greek Government should know, I shall tell them.'

'Then I can't tell you what I wanted to tell you. I promised I would keep the information to myself.'

Worried, I sought out Robert Kennedy again. 'All kinds of unsubstantiated information is reaching Washington,' I said. 'Greeks like Andreas Papandreou are being represented as Communists by your people in Greece. The US might be badly misled by wrong information coming from Greece.'

'There's nothing I can do about it. Lyndon won't listen to me,' said Robert Kennedy.

'But there are men who worked for your brother and are now working for Johnson. They might listen to you.'

'How do I know you are not misleading me?' asked Robert Kennedy.

'I hoped you might trust me.'

'I trusted you as a journalist. Can I trust you now that you work for the Greek Government?'

'I do work for the Greek Government, Mr Kennedy. And this Government is not crazy. It is not Communist. It is not anti-American. It simply wants a little more dignity than it is allowed in its dealings with America. There isn't even a threat I can utter: I can't say that Greece will turn to Russia if the Americans continue treating us as they do. We are your friends and allies. We will remain your allies. I would also like us to remain your friends.'

'There's nothing I can do,' said Kennedy. 'There's nothing I can do. I'm sorry.'

In Greece, the sense of imminent doom increased. General Grivas kept up his passionate warnings against the mythical ASPIDA plot through which Andreas Papandreou would deliver the Greek army to the Communists.

The Americans in Greece talked overtly of a justifiable coup to save Greece from that dangerous leftist, Papandreou. Even Cy Sulzberger, the chief foreign correspondent of the *New York Times*, began writing that to save Greece, its young King might suspend the constitution.

On July 15, 1965, King Constantine of Greece dismissed the Cabinet of George Papandreou. Some time later, Marguerite Higgins called me:

'I'm sorry I did not tell you what I knew when last we met. I wanted to give you three names: Papadopoulos, Makarezos, Roufagalis. They are Greek officers connected one way or another with intelligence. They are our most prized sources in Greece. If I'd told you, maybe your Prime Minister could have done something.'

'I doubt it, Marguerite,' I said. 'But thanks all the same.'

King Constantine gave orders for the return to Athens of the members of the future junta who had been sent to provincial commands by the Papandreou Cabinet.[25] Papadopoulos came to the General Staff to take over the psychological warfare bureau. Makarezos was appointed to a controlling position in the Greek CIA. Pattakos was brought back and given command of the armoured forces in the Athens region. Spandidakis became Chief of Staff.

From his position in the General Staff, Papadopoulos covered the country with rumours. 'Evidence' of sabotage was discovered here, there and everywhere. Today it was a bridge that was going to be blown up. Tomorrow it was three thousand rifles imported and distributed to Communists in Euboia: the actual figure was eighty-two shotguns bought by hunters and duly registered with the police.[26]

Several newspapers which actively supported the junta later, carried stories daily about the disintegration of the country, the growing Communist subversion, the imminent collapse of law and order. At the trial of the junta, in August 1975, every major witness was asked whether there was such a danger of collapse. The answer was a unanimous 'no', an answer given by people who served as Cabinet Ministers and were opponents of Papandreou, by the chiefs of the armed services in the period immediately preceding the coup, by a whole parade of generals.

Here is the testimony given at the junta trial on July 30, 1975, by Mr Canellopoulos, Prime Minister at the time of the coup and opponent of George Papandreou:

'All the rumours about the instability of the situation were lies, lies that were circulated for two to two and a half years before the coup and by which I too was duped (for a time) . . .

'Information was being given to the Government, to the King and to me as head of a political party . . . information that weapons had been gathered by the Communists . . . that a night of St Bartholomew was being prepared . . . Already, by the end of 1965 I was certain that all these things were lies. I had the opportunity to write a report to the King in January 1966 in which I spoke of the dangers the country faced not from the Communists but from the people who were spreading all this false information. I spoke categorically in that report to the King of pressures tending to the overthrow of the Constitution. And naturally, I told him that this should never be allowed to happen.'

The Americans knew that a coup was in the offing. At a White House meeting in February 1967, Professor Walt Rostow, who handled the business of the National Security Council declared that Greece was headed towards an overthrow of the Constitution and that the US should not intervene.[28] For nearly two years after he overthrew Prime Minister Papandreou, and by setting up one short-lived Cabinet after another (they all failed to obtain votes of confidence in Parliament), the King tried to avoid holding the elections prescribed by the Constitution, playing for time, in the hope that the Papandreous would lose their popularity. But the popularity of the Papandreous grew daily. It was obvious that only by a coup could they be prevented from winning an election.

The generals the King considered most faithful, planned a coup. It was going to follow the lines laid down in 'Plan Prometheus', the NATO plan for military takeover, in case of emergency. These generals have become known, since, as the 'big junta'. But there was another junta, the 'small junta', made up of Papadopoulos, Makarezos, Pattakos, Roufogalis etc., the colonels and majors who were to do the dirty work for the generals. The 'small junta' struck first and for its own benefit.

In the small hours of April 21st, the colonels occupied the Greek 'Pentagon', the Athens Radio, telecommunications centres. They circled the palace with troops. They arrested all political leaders. General Gregory Spandidakis flashed the codeword 'Prometheus' telling the armed forces to take over. Many commanders phoned from the provinces to inquire whether it was General Spandidakis, himself, who had ordered the execution of 'Prometheus'; he assured them that it was indeed he who had given the order. Units around the country obeyed. Papadopoulos had the Athens Radio broadcast that the Armed Forces, on instructions from the King, the Prime Minister and the Cabinet, had taken over.[27]

Still, there was danger for the junta. There were officers, senior to the members of the junta and commanders of military units who might refuse to accept the authority of a group of obscure colonels and majors who were widely considered by their superiors as overzealous fanatics. The junta badly needed a royal blessing.

Before giving his blessing, the King asked to talk to Prime Ministers Canellopoulos. They were both, at the time, at the 'Pentagon', more or less prisoners of the junta. Here is what went on, in the words of Mr Canellopoulos' testimony given at the junta's trial on July 30, 1975:

'The King asked me what I thought he should do. And I answered: There are two solutions. In one of the two solutions you will find me by your side. It is this. You should immediately call those who are in charge to gather all the officers, here in the great hall of the Pentagon . . . There you should tell those primarily responsible to put themselves at your disposal. And you should tell the rest that you forgive them and that you want them to go back to their units. In such circumstances, I shall do my duty and stand beside you up to the time when what I propose will have succeeded, whereupon I shall resign because it was during my tenure of office that this great calamity occurred.

'The other solution, I said to the King, was to make a deal. "But in that case you will no longer be King I shall not be by your side . . ." The King did not accept the first solution because he said he wanted to avoid bloodshed . . . There were many officers in the building who would not have followed those who stand accused today . . . The King said to me then, "I think of giving the premiership to Mr Kollias." I replied that since he had taken his decision, I would leave and I left.'

Mr Kollias, of course, was the chief prosecutor who tried to block the investigation of the murder of Gregory Lambrakis.

There followed considerable haggling between the junta and the King on the makeup of the government he would swear in. This has been described in detail at the trial of the junta. The King won one point, that Mr Kollias be the Prime Minister. George Papadopoulos, the strongman of the junta was appointed 'Minister to the Prime Minister', and it was he who ruled. In the next few days, the King signed a series of decrees retiring from the Armed Forces senior officers who would have defended him against the junta.[29] The King's praetorian guard had done what praetorian guards always do: it took away his power. Those who do not read history are condemned to repeat it, Santayana says.

I received a message from Robert Kennedy. He said that he was sorry.

Dean Acheson, formerly US Secretary of State, formerly the lawyer representing a Greek democratic government, wrote to the *Washington Post* protesting against criticism of the Greek junta: Greece, said he, was not ready for democracy; maybe Britain was, the Scandinavians, the Benelux countries and, of course, the United States.

I had a conversation with Mr Acheson; he called me on the

phone to complain about letters I had written to the newspapers countering his arguments. I kept careful notes of the conversations—as a journalist I had long practice in quick note-taking.

'My dear fellow,' said the great lawyer, 'you shouldn't act like that. You can't possibly dispute the fact that your country is not ready for democracy. All this cradle of democracy stuff is based on nothing: Thucydides himself said about the regime of Pericles that it was a democracy only in name but in fact it was the rule of the best man. Modern Greece hasn't had a chance to learn about democracy. How old is your country now? One hundred and forty years old? And you've spent most of those years in wars to liberate those Greeks who were still under Turkish domination. Democracy is a skill to acquire by practice. You have not had enough practice.'

'We were giving it a try, Mr Acheson,' I said, 'until the King ousted Prime Minister Papandreou. And now we have a military dictatorship. You know, as well as I do, that the US could have prohibited that coup.'

'What would such an American intervention have meant?' Mr Acheson asked. 'Would not such intervention have been a breach of Greece's independence? There was nothing we could do. Your officer corps decided that there was too much political instability and moved to stop that state of affairs.'

'The officer corps would not have dared to move had the US indicated it did not want a coup, and you know that as well as I do Mr Acheson. I feel that you have stolen my country.'

'My dear fellow,' said Mr Acheson, 'you are being preposterous. We did not steal your country. It is still run by Greeks.'

'By Greeks who were trained by your Central Intelligence Agency; by Greeks who have been your main sources of information in Greece. You stole my country, Mr Acheson.'

'No stealing took place,' said the former and ageing Secretary of State. 'At most, someone might try to make a case that we purchased your country. It was offered for sale by the Greeks.'

'Greeks your money debauched, Mr Acheson.'

'Oh dear, you have become melodramatic, haven't you? I used to think you rather sensible when you were a journalist.'

'Do you remember an article I once wrote, in which I mentioned you, Mr Acheson? The article about Diwali, the Hindu festival? I had written that an Indian merchant had fashioned two devils, one in Stalin's likeness and one in yours. He told me that being a neutralist, he thought you and Stalin were as bad as the other. You have been shocked, if I remember your words. I am beginning to think that Indian was not far from the truth.'

The former Secretary of State was angered. In beautifully chiselled sentences he listed all the errors in my reasoning. 'Stalin,' he concluded, 'was sanguinary. I have not caused one drop of Greek blood to be shed. US troops did not march into your country as Russian troops marched into Hungary. We have lavished our wealth on Greece. We protected you. You should cherish us. There is no comparison with the Russians in which we do not come out as benevolent friends and they as brutal tyrants.'

'If you want me to say that you are better than the Russians, Mr Acheson, I shall say it readily. But it is faint praise. Compared with what I was taught you stood for, you come out sadly lacking.'

'Surely you are not going to quote me George Washington on foreign entanglements,' said Mr Acheson. 'This is the twentieth century, you know. America is a great power. It is a role we could not have evaded. This role has its own logic. If we ignore such logic the world can either fall into anarchy or into the hands of Russia. We are the leaders of the free world.'

'And it does not strike you as odd that all your allies who receive direct military aid from you are military dictatorships, from Latin America all the way to South Korea?'

'All such countries, including yours, are at the stage in their political evolution when democracy cannot yet work. Your choice is between, on the one hand, rule by the Greek army and the Greek establishment and, on the other hand, by Greek puppets of Moscow. You remember the atrocities the Greek Communists committed?'

'So for us, the small, there cannot be the middle way. Is that what you are saying, Mr Acheson? It is either the extreme right or the extreme left?'

'It is not we, the Americans, who have posed this dilemma: it is the Communists. Blame them, not us. We just play the role history has thrust upon us. We defend the free world and we cannot afford to make mistakes in Greece.'

'In a very real sense, Mr Acheson, what you have done to Greece is unforgivable. You have bought the Greeks and paid handsomely and so you have deprived us even of the nobility of hating you as the Hungarians and the Czechs hate the Russians.'

'If you could hear yourself talk,' said the former American Secretary of State, 'you would be thankful, as I am, that Greece isn't run by vague intellectuals such as you. Our talk has only affirmed my belief that in Greece there was no realistic alternative to your colonels.' He banged the phone.

Other than the facts that I have given above, what evidence is there of complicity by the Lyndon Johnson government in the coup which overthrew Greek democracy on April 21, 1967? Greek investigating judges are looking into the case currently (early 1975), taking sworn testimony, cross-checking it. Gradually, it is being released to the press. Here are some items.

Colonel Antonios Papaspyrou (rtd) states that in the spring of 1965, at the Metropolis Hotel in Kozani, a town in northern Greece, he met a US colonel whom he had long known and the colonel said that he considered as the only suitable leader for Greece Colonel George Papadopoulos. (Source, a letter from Colonel Papaspyrou to the Greek newspaper *TO VIMA*, to which he has made available the name of the US colonel.) Be it noted that at the time this conversation took place, the King had not yet ousted the Papandreou government. The US colonel also expressed the view that all Greek politicians were worthless.

Several of the investigations now being carried out by judges in Greece have uncovered that many years before the coup, members of the junta not only had been trained by the American CIA but were salaried employees of the American CIA. This information has also been given in the *New York Times* in an article distributed by its news service on August 2, 1974. The *New York Times* quotes two US officials as saying that Papadopoulos was among the many military and political figures in Greece who were receiving personal stipends from the CIA for many years. Another source quoted by the same *New York Times* article says that Papadopoulos was in the pay of the CIA continuously since 1952.

There is sworn testimony by a member of KYP (the Greek CIA) that some American CIA members, wearing Greek uniforms, participated in the coup on the night of April 21st, 1974 to make sure it would be bloodless. How much credence can one give testimony from an intelligence agent, whatever his nationality? At any rate, if there were such US participation, it was, at least, for a laudable purpose : to prevent the shedding of blood.

Are these items enough evidence together with the evidence

I gave before that there was American complicity in the coup? Most of the investigating judges in Greece seem convinced by the documentation they have compiled that there was such complicity. I visited Greece in November 1974 and leading politicians to whom I spoke were also convinced of such complicity. They all said that for the sake of preserving good relations with the US, the evidence on US complicity will not be made fully public.

We have seen that in February 1967, the White House itself raised no objections to the coup by the generals, the so-called 'big junta'. Did the White House know about the coup that the 'small junta'—Papadopoulos and company—were preparing? There is no evidence on this, one way or another. That American officers serving in Greece knew about the plans of Papadopoulos seems fairly well established by the evidence now being collected by Greek investigating judges. Is it possible that the superiors of those American officers were told nothing by their well-informed subordinates and that, if the superiors were told, that they, in turn, said nothing to Mr Rusk or Mr Johnson? These are questions that may have to wait for an answer.

Incidentally, the US government, and the British government for that matter, accorded diplomatic recognition to the junta with unseemly haste: within a week, both Washington and London had recognised the new regime, had recognised the over-throw of democracy in a member of NATO, an alliance set up to defend democracy.

The King, of course, went along with the coup. It was not exactly the coup he had wanted: these were not his friendly generals and courtiers taking power, but a group of hitherto unknown and unnoticed colonels and majors. Still, they professed ferocious anti-Communism and they were going to prevent the elections that would have brought Papandreou back to power with an increased majority. And a Papandreou electoral victory would have meant that the Greek people sided with Papandreou who wanted the army to be under the control of the elected parliament and not under the control of the King.

How did the colonels rule Greece?

There hardly is an area of national life which they did not worsen. To have the right to teach, teachers had to attend schools of political indoctrination and had to teach children that the coup had saved the country from Communism and had begun the 'third Greek civilisation', (the other two civilisations being those of ancient Greece and of the Byzantine empire). Teachers were appointed without qualifications other than loyalty to the junta. They spied on their more professional colleagues. Thousands of competent teachers were fired. The students, by the way, were so disgusted that they became prey to the Communist party, the only one that knew how to survive underground: at the university elections in November 1974, the Communist students won by a huge landslide, in an election in which nearly all students voted.

The man appointed President of the University of Salonika was an admirer of Nazi Germany. He stayed there when Italy attacked Greece in World War II—he did not return to fight for his country. Letters he had written to friends in Greece, praising Nazi Germany, have been published. The appointment was not surprising considering that George Papadopoulos himself, after the Germans invaded Greece, joined the so-called 'Security Battalions' whose main task was to track down Greek resistance fighters.

But these are the small demeanours of the junta.

They came in proclaiming they would cleanse the country of political corruption yet, daily, evidence of corruption under the junta is piling up.

There was a bank in Greece, created before the junta, called the National Bank for Industrial Development. It turns out that the bank is now on its knees and must be rescued by the government. An official audit of the bank's books shows that relatives of the junta were given loans which no sane banker would ever have given, for enterprises that turned out to be on a much smaller scale than the plans presented to the bank. In other words, much less was invested in the enterprise than the bank had been led to believe. What happened to the rest of the money? I know of my knowledge, because I saw it with my own eyes, that in one such instance, a Greek employee was forced by a member of the junta to carry one million dollars abroad to deposit in a numbered bank account. The employee was told that if he did not do so, he would be fired and all his relatives would be fired. This man has begged me not to reveal his name because he did, in fact, commit an illegal act and is afraid.

How can one explain the contract between the Greek junta and a US firm called MACDONALD? This US firm contracted to build a road and received $40 million for the job. The firm delivered a segment of road costing $2.5 million, that's all.

The contract with the Macdonald company provided guarantees TO THE COMPANY, NOT TO THE GREEK GOVERN-MENT. Whatever happened, Macdonald would collect. The Minister of Public Works in the civilian government which succeeded the junta, after examining the documents of the case, expressed his astonishment to the Greek press on September 25, 1974:

'For the first time in the history of modern Greece, it was not the contractor who had to guarantee the performance of his task, by presenting written guarantees, but the state (the junta) that the contract would not be annulled, no matter what.' The matter is sub-judice and no more can be said about the reasons why such money-conscious men as the junta members signed such a contract.

The total effects on the Greek economy of the seven junta years (when trains ran on time and monuments were built as so many visitors to Greece were wont to say after a week or two on the beaches during their vacations) were summarised on August 23, 1974 by Mr John Pesmatzoglou, the minister of finance in the civilian government which took over when the junta fell:

'The budget presented (by the junta) in November 1973 was a lie. To create the impression of frugality, revenue and expenses were recorded as different to those that had in reality been calculated. Nine and one half billion drachmas (317 million US dollars) in expenses were not shown in the budget. (The sum may not seem enormous to Canadians, Britons or Americans but they should remember that for Greece, a very poor country, this is indeed a huge sum.) And these hidden expenses had reached 780 million dollars by the time the junta fell—expenses not shown in the budget. In other words, 30% of the total expenditures had not been shown in the budget. There are great deficits in the accounts of the government with the Bank of Greece and no provisions for covering these deficits. The audit does not include the accounts of semi-private and crown corporations. The public debt tripled during the seven years of the junta's rule. The public debt in foreign currency—money owed abroad—quadrupled in the seven years of the junta's rule.'

And now we must pass to the most horrifying aspect of the junta's rule, its brutality.

The junta was composed of brutal men. One of them, for instance, John Ladas, was in charge of the ministry of the interior.

Cy Sulzberger, of the *New York Times*, in a series of articles he has written on the junta SINCE ITS FALL recounts the following episode: A Greek magazine called Eikones, wrote an article on homosexuality through the ages and included mention of the practice among the Greeks. Ladas ordered the three principal editors of the magazine brought to his office and beat them up personally.

Now that the junta has fallen, proof of its brutality can be documented. The victims have spoken and even their torturers have confessed, pleading that they were ordered to perform their grisly tasks.

Let us start with the least horrible aspects of the junta, its choice of the island in which the colonels imprisoned those who incurred their displeasure, the infamous island of Yaros. It has now been emptied of its inmates and thoroughly inspected; here is what Yaros was like, according to 42 Greeks and foreign journalists who visited the island on August 2, 1974. It should be said that right wing governments preceding the junta had used Yaros as Greece's Devil's Island since 1947.

The prison itself was built by the inmates in 1947 on a plan provided by a British officer whose name was Wickham (I am transliterating back into English from a Greek document and the spelling of the English officer's name may be wrong. His Christian name is not given). It has three floors and a basement for those in solitary confinement. It is a building open to the winds and unheated.

Enormous rats, in their thousands, roam the prison, feeding on the piles of garbage which the guards would not allow to be removed. The most common injury in Yaros was to be bitten by rats, in one's sleep. Prisoners lost parts of their ears, noses or even fingers. No effort was ever made to exterminate the rats. They were part of the punishment. Several inmates contracted rabies from rat bites. There was a 'hospital', a semi-ruined house with some straw on the floor for the sick to lie on.

For the last eight months of their stay on Yaros, the inmates only ate plain boiled macaroni, every day.

Here is the testimonial of Stathis Panagoulis, one of the Yaros inmates:

'Before they sent me to Yaros they put me in a prison cell (in Attica). I was freezing and asked for a blanket. They said they would warm me and they beat me for a whole hour with a bull-whip. At ten o'clock at night they asked me again if I was cold and they began beating me again. The next day they did not beat me but they did not give me anything to eat or drink. The day following they gave me some bread and then they began beating me again until I lost consciousness. I stayed in that cell seven days and they gave me beatings each day. Then they said I was free. They made me sign the release papers. They opened the door and let me take five steps into the courtyard, then four guards grabbed me and manacled me . . .'

He was taken from prison to prison, always in underground cells. Eventually he was sent to Yaros. 'There is no water on Yaros,' Panagoulis continues, 'not a tree. Water is brought once a month from Piraeus. The rats are big as cats and you must have a stick to protect yourself. And the snakes, big black ones nearly three feet long and vipers. I killed at least twenty in my bed over the months. And the scorpions—they're the worst because if they sting you, you really suffer . . . 60 people died from lack of medical care. The only medicine was aspirin. From 1967, 7,000 people were sent to Yaros, 500 of them women.' They were packed like sardines in their cells and at night, the guards would come to watch the women undress. At no time was Stathis Panagoulis told what the charges against him were.

Nikiforos Mandilaras, a brilliant Greek lawyer, who had defended the accused in the trial for the mythical ASPIDA plot and had made a fool of the prosecution, was found dead from drowning, after the junta took over, his body washed ashore on the island of Rhodes. The man the junta claimed to be responsible, a sea captain, has since 'committed suicide'. Maybe it was an accident. But what happened to Anastasios Minis, a Greek war hero in the air force was not an accident. He has recounted his one hundred and eleven days of torture at the hands of the infamous ESA (the initials stand for Greek Military Police) for activities against the junta. Mr Minis had let off bombs, of his own manufacture, placing them carefully, always, to avoid wounding anyone. He was thus, undoubtedly, guilty of unlawful behaviour. He acted alone, was not a member of any organisation. He was offered a choice : to collaborate with the junta for a fancy sum of money, or suffer the consequences. His arrest had been noted in the foreign press.

He refuses to collaborate with the junta. He subsequently is taken to a hospital and given a thorough medical check-up. He

129

is kept in solitary confinement for several days then is allowed to see his wife in the presence of a guard.

After that meeting he is taken back to his cell where he is visited by two guards. One says 'get up, fuck your virgin mary you bastard.' He is then ordered to stand up, three feet from the wall and facing the wall, at attention. They then remove his bed from his cell and bring in a card table and chair plus writing material. He is told he can stop standing at attention only to sit down to write the names of all those in his organisation. Minis answers that there is no organisation to write about. He is now supervised by one guard who keeps telling him to stand more rigidly at attention. Two hours later, Minis is still standing. A new guard called Tsoumis comes in who notices that Minis is not unsteady on his feet and sweating and tells him 'you will melt like a candle unless you do as you are told. Write for your own good or you won't come out alive.'

Minis is still kept standing. He asks for water but is not given any. It is night by now. He has been standing since noon. At midnight he falls unconscious. A doctor is fetched to examine him and orders orange juice. Minis is then allowed to sit but a guard prevents him from falling asleep. The next morning, the doctor orders that Minis be given food and drink. Minis is allowed to sleep till noon and is then taken to the office of Major Nicolas Hadjizisis who is in charge.

'Minis,' says Major Hadjizisis, 'we're going to make you talk. I don't care if your pulse drops to 45 or 30 or zero.'[30]

Minis is taken back to his cell, made to stand at attention three feet from the wall again. The guard Tsoumis asks:

'Will you write?'

'I have nothing to write.'

Tsoumis then begins beating Minis with a club. Minis fights Tsoumis who calls for help. Minis is made to stand again and the guard Tsoumis resumes the beating, striking him on the calves, thighs and buttocks. They draw a circle on the floor, forty centimetres in diameter and it is in that circle that Minis has to stand. Guards change every two and a half hours during the day and every one hour and a half during the night. Minis is standing in his green circle being constantly beaten. He has hallucinations.

The next day, another guard, Vangellis Mavropoulos, allows Minis to sit and smoke a cigarette and to drink some water. There is another guard present, Nicolas Papaioannou who never struck Minis. After the cigarette, Minis is made to stand again in the green circle. Six more days pass with Minis standing and being beaten. His feet are so swollen that they burst his shoes. Then another kind guard comes in and lets Minis sit, 'but don't tell anyone I let you sit or they'll courtmartial me,' cautions the guard. 'If they ask you who treated you the worst, tell them it is me, the one with the teeshirt with the motorcycle on the front.' (This guard's name was Vlassis Andrikopoulos. He has since corroborated the details of Minis' torture.) Minis came to wait anxiously for the time when this guard would be on watch because he was never beaten by him nor made to stand.

On the tenth day (July 10, 1972) Minis is officially allowed to sit, and given tea; and a succession of captains comes to interrogate him. Minis knows the names of only two, Bellos and Tsalas. He keeps telling them that there are no members of his 'organisation' whose names he can reveal. He is then allowed a rest which lasts from July 11th to the 17th.

On the 17th of July, Colonel Demetrios Ioannidis, the commander of ESA (the Greek Military Police) himself interrogates Minis. Ioannidis, after some small talk says:

'You have realised by now that the human being, for us, is of secondary or tertiary importance. I shall give you 24 hours more to think.' Then Ioannidis adds, smiling, 'after that, if you do not collaborate with us, certain organs of your body may become totally useless, though at your age they are already becoming useless.'

Minis is given more than 24 hours: from the 18th through the 28th of July he is not tortured. He is even allowed to see his wife for ten minutes in the presence of a guard. On the evening of July 29, Major Hadjizisis orders Minis to write everything about his activities—whom he has met, talked to, lunched with. Minis returns to his cell and writes 12 pages on four trips abroad he had taken in previous years.

At ten o'clock the next morning, July 30th, he is again visited by doctor Demetrios Papadopoulos who had given him his initial checkup. The doctor inquires about Minis' health and says he will order better food and soft drinks. At noon, Minis is taken to the office of a major whose name, he thinks, is Oikonomopoulos.

'You have been making fools of us with what you have written. We have treated you well till now but now this is over.'

Minis is taken back to his cell which is now empty of all

furniture. He is ordered to stand at attention and a guard begins to beat him with a club on the calves, thighs and buttocks, varying this with punches to the abdomen. The beating is accompanied by continuous blaspheming. This guard is succeeded by another who continues the beating, adding now violent slaps on either side of Minis' face. A second guard comes in and Minis is being beaten by two men. He faints. They drag him to a tap outside his cell and turn on the water to bring him back to his senses. The beating continues. The guards bring glasses of water and pour them on the floor, holding the glass some inches away from Minis' mouth. He falls down and they beat him as he lays prone, kicking him, and beating the soles of his feet with their clubs. Finally, he seems in such bad shape that the guards stop the beating and begin massaging his heart. They bring back his cot on July 31st and let him lie. The doctor comes, inspects him and prescribes some orange juice.

For some days Minis is not tortured. He is again allowed to see his wife. Then, Minis meets Major Hadjizisis who says: 'What are we going to do with you? Don't you understand that we are not going to get tired. We shall torture you three months, six months, one year, until we get you to talk.' Minis repeats that he has nothing to reveal, that he has no accomplices.

He is taken back to his cell and put in the hands of a guard called Demos, the cruellest. He begins beating Minis who counterattacks and Demos calls for help. Two guards rush in to help, and they beat Minis, all three, for some time, then they leave him, weakened, to the tender mercies of Demos who not only uses his club but punches Minis in the stomach, knees him in the groin and stamps hard on the prisoner's toes, varying this with slaps to the head. Demos is the biggest of the guards and the strongest, 6 feet 4 inches tall. Demos' watch ends and he replaced by another guard called Heracles who moonlights as a boxer. The beating continues. Minis vomits repeatedly. He tries to kill himself by rushing at the wall to smash his head. He bleeds now profusely but the beating continues through the night. The trick of pouring glasses of water on the floor before Minis who is dying of thirst also continues. July 19, July 20, July 21, the beating continues.

Minis howls that he will confess everything. They let him write and he describes an imaginary conspiracy with fictitious names and addresses of his non-existent collaborators. The stratagem is uncovered and the torture continues . . .

Why go on describing the bestiality? Minis spent 111 days in the hands of ESA. I have written the above to pay tribute to the incredible courage of the man and to the equally incredible endurance of the human body.

Minis was not the only victim. There were hundreds, thousands even, who went through this sort of treatment for varying periods. Many were crippled for life, like Colonel Spyridon Moustaklis, another war hero, holder of the Greek equivalent of the Victoria Cross or, in American terms, the Congressional Medal of Honour. He was taken from his home in May 1973—this was not his first arrest. Fifty days later, his wife was allowed to see him in a military hospital. He bore the signs of cigarette burns on his right shoulder, his forearms, his genitals. The soles of his feet were a raw pulp (beating on the soles of the feet was a favourite procedure of the junta). He could not keep his head upright. His right side was paralysed and he had lost the power of speech. Now that the junta has fallen, doctors are trying to repair some of the damage done to Moustaklis. But he will never fully recover either the use of his right side or of his speech because one of the tortures they inflicted upon him consisted of having one guard pull his head to the back and to the side by the hair, while another hit his exposed and twisted neck with a club.[31]

And there was the use of tanks and machine guns against unarmed protesting students of the Athens Polytechnic University in November 1973, with many deaths.

Did the Americans in Greece know what was going on? The CIA in Greece before the coup on April 21, 1967, had 60 members on its official staff. Papadopoulos and hundreds of agents of KYP (the Greek CIA) were trained by the Americans in anti-terrorist and interrogation techniques. We have seen that documentary evidence has been uncovered that KYP employees were in the pay of the Americans. The Americans had offices available to them in the buildings of KYP and ESA. The closest collaboration existed between American intelligence services and their Greek counterparts.

Foreign journalists knew of the tortures that were being inflicted. Cyrus Sulzberger, the distinguished chief of correspondents for the *New York Times*, knew about it, as he has said in his series of articles written since the fall of the junta. Stories about torture, documented stories, citing names, appeared in the European press throughout the seven years of the junta's rules.

Is it credible that James Pott, Chief of the CIA in Greece and his agents did not know what their good friends of the junta were doing in the torture chambers? And did none of these stories ever reach the ears of Lyndon Johnson or Richard Nixon?

Yet US support for the junta was unflagging. Writing in the London *Observer* of July 1, 1973, Charles Foley quotes Henry Taska, the US ambassador to Greece at the time, saying approvingly of the junta that the colonels were the most anti-Communist team one could find anywhere; that there was no country like Greece which offered the US such facilities and as much support as did the junta. Maurice Stans, US Secretary of Commerce and chief fund-raiser for Mr Nixon's electoral battles, visited Greece and officially expressed Mr Nixon's admiration for the country's progress. US Foreign Secretary Rogers celebrated the fourth of July 1972, in Greece, with the junta. Vice-President Agnew made a triumphal official visit to Greece and repeatedly praised the junta. Mr Agnew's principal vade-mecum in Greece was, of course, Tom Pappas, the Greek American businessman mentioned in the Watergate tapes.

All this US support for a government that stole, tortured and mismanaged during a period when the Human Rights Commission of the Council of Europe officially condemned the Greek junta for ignoring the international agreement on human rights by committing torture.

The last act is perhaps the most grotesque. A coup within the junta topples Papadopoulos and replaces him with the arch-torturer of Minis and the other victims of the dictatorship, Demetrios Ioannides, the graduate of American training on anti-subversive techniques. The Prime Minister named by Ioannides is a Greek-American, A. Androutsopoulos, who came to Greece after World War Two as an official employee of the United States Central Intelligence Agency, a fact of which Mr Androutsopoulos has often boasted.

Then came the tragic denouement. Ioannidis, megalomaniac and surely no more mentally balanced than torturers usually are, organises a coup against President Makarios of Cyprus.

A *New York Times* news service dispatch from Washington published by *TO VIMA* in Athens on August 11, 1974, suggests that the Americans knew of Ioannides' projected coup in Cyprus and that Washington's reaction had been mild enough not to dissuade Ioannides. The State Department does not deny that US employees in Greece had heard Ioannides' views on a coup against Makarios. According to the *New York Times*, advice was sent that no such coup be attempted but no threats were attached to the advice—no mention was made of stopping US aid.

To attempt a coup in Cyprus against Makarios was, of course, worse than criminal: it was sheer idiocy. To replace Makarios as President by Nikos Sampson, a notorious terrorist and declared partisan of ENOSIS, the union of Cyprus with Greece, was to give Turkey the pretext for which it had long waited, to invade Cyprus and take the richest and only economically viable part of the island.

Is it significant that for three days after the coup in Cyprus, the State Department did not express disapproval of the coup and that at the UN Security Council, the US blocked moves to condemn the coup in Cyprus? The US was not fond of Makarios' neutralism even though, for the preservation of Cyprus' unity, Makarios had to be neutralist, hoping that if he did not align himself with the Greeks—and therefore with the Americans—Russia would discourage any Turkish invasion of Cyprus, to keep all Cyprus out of NATO.

Finally, the Turks invaded and the US did nothing to dissuade them. Mr Kissinger accepted the new solution: should one surmise that it gave him the eventual hope of a military base much closer to Israel than any other base available to US forces? That is surmise. But in asking for military aid to the Greek junta once, Mr Nixon had said: 'Without aid to Greece, we would not have a viable policy for saving Israel.'

Israel deserves, indeed, to be saved. It is a brave and beleaguered nation. But the Greeks in the street ask themselves whether Israel had to be saved at the expense of Cyprus, and, during the seven years of dictatorship, at the expense of liberty in Greece. But that may not be a reflection of the facts: it may only be an expression of the bitterness Greeks feel at having seen America so actively support and praise the torturers of Greece during seven years, even making available a US radio transmitting station in Greece for the broadcast of junta propaganda to the Greek people.

(At hearings of a subcommittee on foreign relations of the US House of Representatives, in April 1974, the spokesman for the United States Information Agency, Mr Gildner, admitted that its broadcasting facilities at Kavalla in Northern Greece were made available for a considerable number of hours each day to the junta. A congressman asked what the American people would think on learning that facilities built with their tax dollars were used to broadcast the propaganda of a dictatorial regime.)

But as the distinguished American correspondent Stanley Carnow wrote, when the junta had created the Cyprus crisis and the US made no move to stop the Turkish invasion, it is tragic to be a small country in the age of Henry Kissinger.

And so, having emptied the national coffers, having set back Greek education to the state that preceded the enlightenment in the 18th century, having tortured and imprisoned thousands of innocent Greeks, the colonels proved themselves to be inept even in military matters. They launched a mad adventure which could only lead to Turkish military intervention in Cyprus. Then they got frightened and gave up power, because the Cyprus crisis had forced them to mobilise the army and they could not control the thousands of armed reservists as they had controlled an unarmed population.

The Greek people now are free. They voted in free elections and showed themselves to be anything but the wild radical mob whose free expression of political will had to be suppressed by the coup the 'big junta', the generals, were preparing, a coup that Lyndon Johnson's adviser and Lyndon Johnson himself knew about and which they decided not to stop.

With a civilian government in power, there remained only the question of the monarchy. Should the King be brought back, or should Greece become a republic? It had always astonished me, while I was in Greece, to find how royalist the Americans were. The then American Ambassador, Henry Labouisse, asked me to arrange an occasional lunch between him and the King because that would improve Labouisse's image in the State Department. I could hardly believe my ears. Henry Labouisse, former high UN official, begging for an invitation to the palace. Other American officials, on meeting the King simpered—there is no other word for it.

Ever since the flight of the King from Greece in late 1967 and until the junta fell, the great American republic was pressing the junta to bring back the King. I had once seen a George Bernard Shaw comedy in which the US had voted to put itself back under the British crown and I remember a scene in which the stage King of England listens with consternation as the American ambassador announces the decision of both houses of Congress and declares that he will have the pleasure and honour to visit

His Majesty, the next day, in court dress. In Athens, all Americans seemed dying to get into court dress.

But the Greek people are no longer royalist. They have had enough of foreign royal families imposed on Greece by foreign powers to find a job for some princeling related to Queen Victoria and a particular King of Denmark with a huge progeny.

Greek Kings always acted as despots and threw out all Prime Ministers who did not accept the royal will unquestioningly, even though those Prime Ministers may have had overwhelming majorities behind them. King Constantine the First, in the First World War accepted a forty million gold mark loan from Germany, a loan that was intended for the Greek exchequer but never got there and he threw out the pro-entente Greek Prime Minister who had won the elections with a huge majority. (Source: documents of the German foreign office from the First World War. See Appendix D.) From the same source, we find a letter from King Constantine, who had by then been thrown out of Greece, urging the Kaiser to launch an offensive, together with Bulgaria, against Greece. King Constantine volunteered to lead this offensive against what was supposed to be his country.

Constantine the First was restored while Greece was embroiled in a war with Turkey. He immediately fired the skilled, battle-tested generals who were winning battles for Greece and replaced them with courtiers; one of them, the new commander-in-chief, General Hadjanestis believed that one of his legs was made of fragile glass and his chief concern was to prevent it from breaking.

Again in the dossiers of the German foreign ministry, we read correspondence between the principal military adviser, of Constantine I, General John Metaxas, and the German military attaché in Athens on organising the assassination of Eleftherios Venizelos, the Greek Liberal Prime Minister who opposed the King's desire to help Germany in World War One.

Twenty years later, King George II makes General John Metaxas dictator of Greece. Incidentally, there had been several assassination attempts against Venizelos, the most notorious being carried out in the early 1930's by the chief of the Athens Police, Mr Polychronopoulos and Greece's public enemy number one, Karanthanassis, both standing in an open Buick and firing at Venizelos' car with tommy guns. Polychronopoulos remained an honoured member of the palace clique.

We have already discussed the habits of Queen Mother

Frederika. Her son's responsibility for the overthrow of democracy has now been established at the junta trial.

Daily, under the junta, the King signed decrees brought to him by Papadopoulos, the real head of the junta, consolidating the junta's power and dismissing from the armed forces some of the King's most loyal supporters.

In the middle of October 1967, in a telephone call to his father-in-law, the King of Denmark, King Constantine tells of his plan for a counter-coup against the junta. This fact was revealed by King Frederick of Denmark to Prince Peter of Greece. On October 28, George Papadopoulos says to King Constantine : 'Majesty, do not try a counter-coup because it will fail and it will be to your detriment.' King Constantine had not thought that Papadopoulos would have bugged the palace phones!

Prince Peter of Greece adds that all NATO countries have interconnected electronic surveillance systems and the system recorded the conversation between the two Kings. When it became known in Denmark that NATO snoops were bugging the telephone conversations of King Frederick himself, there were huge demonstrations in Copenhagen and the bugging installations were allegedly removed (source, interview with Prince Peter in *TA NEA*, Athens, November 12, 1974).

King Constantine did not heed Papadopoulos' advice not to try a counter-coup. (Papadopoulos himself corroborates that he gave such advice.) The King launched his counter-coup and it was a pathetic fizzle which gave the junta the chance to discover—through suitable torture of those arrested—which officers in the Greek armed forces had been secret opponents of the junta but had escaped the initial Papadopoulos purges—purges whose orders were signed by the King.

The King went into exile in Rome. Under strong pressure by the Americans, he was not deposed by Papadopoulos—the Americans wanted Greece to remain a monarchy. The King and his family went on collecting their salaries amounting to almost one million dollars annually. He was eventually deposed by Papadopoulos, after another futile attempt at a counter-coup by anti-junta royalists who had escaped the previous purges. Papadopoulos who had made himself viceroy, changed his title to President of the Republic.

Then the junta fell and a Greek government elected by a very large majority which produced a cabinet composed entirely of men with a firm royalist past, held a plebiscite on whether to bring back King Constantine. Seven Greeks out of ten voted no and Greece became a republic.

My father would have enjoyed the irony of seeing the Royal Family he despised expelled by its own supporters. But father had died in 1970. I had my last conversation with him in London where he had gone for treatment. It was a daffodil day. The airport cab left me at a row of tall Palladian mansions converted into flats, surrounding a square full of nannies watching over their fair charges. I would rather have watched children too but I could not postpone my errand. I rang the bell, was admitted and I stood before my father. It was five years since I had seen him last. He still carried more weight than was good for him but he still carried it well and the dressing-gown he wore fell about him like a senatorial toga. There were changes: there was no cigarette—I had never seen him awake and not smoking; and he moved his head to see me with a laboured stretching of the neck, a frown to bring eyes into focus and then, expansively, the smile of welcome.

We gave one another the Mediterranean abbrazzo and there was less strength in his hug than before.

On the transatlantic phone I had spoken to his doctor the day before:

'Your father wants to see you. You must come.'

I searched for words—the precise ones were hard to utter: 'is he . . . is he . . .?'

'He is quite well,' said the doctor's voice. 'Considering that he has cancer of the larynx, ulcers in the stomach and the bladder and that he has survived three coronaries in as many months, he is astoundingly well for a man of 73. But he may not have much time.'

I had come in less than twenty-fours hours and I stood before him looking for changes.

'Have a drink son,' said Lakis Gigantes. 'It is unblended Scotch, a special gift to me from David.' David, a peer of the realm, was one of those who had been in battle at father's side and had worshipped him ever since. 'This is true whisky,' father continued, 'not commercial. Taste it and tell if it's not superb.'

It was not a sunny drink. It tasted as a Scottish island looks in the passing of the day.

'I was hoping you would come sooner, son.'

'I couldn't. I had to study for my doctoral exams.'

'A man must have his sons at his deathbed, and not die in

the street as did your uncle Yanis, to have his eyes closed by strangers' hands.'

'Maybe Yanis had the sort of death he wanted, father.'

'Who would want a premature death, while there's the sky to breathe, and trees, and the sound of friendly voices, and the beautiful earth to see?'

I did not answer. He had always stood for life and it shamed me not to have his will to live, not to have, as he had always had, a deep-felt joy at the taste of good bread, the perfume of a woman, the brilliance of a bloom.

'I wanted you here,' he said, 'because it is many years now that I have not seen you laugh.'

'I laugh often enough, father.'

'With the edge of your lips, as the French say, not with your eyes. You were not this way. You were such a rumbustious merry boy. Now you look tamed.'

'You worry about me unnecessarily. For years, you have only seen me just after a long plane ride, with my time zones and my digestion scrambled. I am not tamed, I'm bilious. But let's talk about you, father.'

In other times, Lakis Gigantes, my father, might have been more than a celebrated hero, admired as a hero even by his ideological enemies. In normal times, there would have been a peacetime sequel to his wartime saga. As it was, his segment of the Greek Liberal party never garnered enough votes for Lakis Gigantes to be elected. And so he lived on after World War Two as a historical legend: even I always thought of him as a legend—a man for whom a posthumous monument had its place chosen while he lived.

Lakis Gigantes had formed and led the third *hieros lochos* in Greek history and freed the Aegean islands, fighting against heavy odds and using tactics that were the stuff of heroic fiction.

Before that, the Sacred Regiment had fought in the desert, one of the long range penetration groups. Once, Montgomery denuded his left flank to strengthen his right wing with which he planned to administer his major blow. Rommel had anticipated this move and had sent a strong tank column to crash through Montgomery's left wing. Only Lakis Gigantes was there, in the desert with his Sacred Regiment. The terrain afforded cover. The men of the Sacred Regiment used everything they had, even blankets: they would hide behind a boulder and stuff a blanket in the tracks of a passing German tank. The tracks would jam, the Germans would open their turret to see what the matter was, and they would be killed by the men of the *hieros lochos*. Eventually, Montgomery sent reinforcements and then came himself. Lakis Gigantes introduced his surviving heroes. 'This,' he said, pointing at a diminutive warrior who looked far too young for his second lieutenant's rank, 'is the best bloody man I've never seen before.'

'Tell me colonel,' Montgomery asked, 'have you never had an English lesson?'

'Yes, I had one once but she had big feet; I never had her again.'

The legend grew apace and Lakis Gigantes became a favourite of the war-correspondents, with his white beard, his pennant cut out of a lady's undergarments, and his brand of English which was vaguely based on the language British Marine sergeants used when training his Sacred Regiment.

The Sacred Regiment was trained to do anything: sweep deep into the desert behind enemy lines; convert to the modern equivalent of Norse seaborne raiders; fall from the sky dangling from parachutes. Lakis Gigantes refused to take the parachute training his men were given. He did not believe he needed any training. So he left for his first action jump, wearing a parachute for the first time. The correspondent of the *Daily Telegraph*, riding in the same plane, wrote that the commander of the Sacred Regiment slept soundly all the way, well prepared because he was carrying spare monocles in the various pockets of his battledress. Why? Because if, perchance, there was a girl on the field of battle, he would prefer to ogle her through a monocle than through unbecoming glasses. He landed safely, his monocle intact, and began tossing hand grenades, his favourite weapon.

He took an island from the Germans and the islanders threw the sort of party that can only happen when an Aegean island has been freed by men falling from the sky. Wine flowed steadily and there was dancing. Lakis Gigantes danced with the best till the music called for a high jump. The young men strove to outdo one another under the approving glances of the village maidens who had unearthed long buried festive costumes for the occasion. And when it was the turn of Lakis Gigantes to jump, he jumped higher than all the others—too high: he fell and broke his thigh.

It was at that moment that Germans from a nearby island

attacked unexpectedly. The commander of the Sacred Regiment was ringed with gourds so he would float and was lowered into a cistern under a floor, with a bottle of brandy to kill the pain. His men retreated, re-formed, annihilated the German force and retrieved their colonel. A signal brought an allied ship and after a passage in a dinghy, Lakis Gigantes was put in a reinforced plaster cast. The next day, he was attacking another island.

He was known as the *geros*, the old man, though he was not the oldest in his unit. There was no limit on age. Youth was not a necessary qualification: the capacity to kill was. One of the best killers, Gyparis, a guerrilla leader in the Cretan wars of independence at the turn of the century, was the best shot of the Sacred Regiment—he could put a bullet through his wedding ring at a hundred paces. He was seventy years old. There were senior naval officers in the regiment, airmen old and young, all volunteers who wanted to serve under Lakis Gigantes.

Once, they captured an entire Italian division on one of the Aegean islands. Some four hundred men of the Sacred Regiment set up what amounted to a fireworks display, using machine-guns, mortars and explosives all rigged to be fired by remote control to give the impression that the Italians were surrounded on all sides. After a suitably impressive show of firepower, Lakis Gigantes sent a herald under flag of truce, bearing a message to the Italian Commander:

'General, you are surrounded, outnumbered and outgunned. You have fought bravely. You have done all that honour demands. It now is your duty to spare the lives of your brave men. You will be accorded the honours of war and allowed to keep your side arms.' It worked. The Italians surrendered.

At other times, Lakis Gigantes, dressed as a fisherman, would hold the tiller of a disreputable looking schooner and would sail in waters patrolled by German coastguard vessels. A German ship would come alongside the schooner and in the next few moments, father's killers, springing from the bowels of their boat, would eliminate the German craft.

The buccaneers of the Sacred Regiment operated from deserted islands off the Turkish coast. Turkish coastguards were bribed lavishly enough to ensure a good postwar life for the bribe taker, provided he agreed to be bribed a sufficient number of times.

Eventually, the Sacred Regiment freed all the Greek Islands in the Aegean and occupied the Dodecanese-Greek islands that had been under Italian rule for many years. Lakis Gigantes became Governor of the islands, ruling from the magnificent medieval fortress the Knights Templar had erected in Rhodes. His was a peaceful fief during the Communist rebellion which began on December 4, 1944 in the rest of Greece. As the ancient ruler of Samos, Polycrates, had once done, Lakis Gigantes struck first: he rounded up all the Communist notables he could find and the wives and children of those he could not find and put them all in a building he surrounded with barbed wire, high explosives and airplane fuel. Should the Communists cause one nose to bleed in the islands Lakis Gigantes proclaimed, the hostages would go up in smoke. There were no nosebleeds, partly because of his threats, partly because the people of the islands felt obligated to him, their liberator, and liked his accessibility, his concern for their welfare, and the justice he meted out from island to island.

On one such occasion, the accused had abandoned a very new wife.

'Why the hell?' asked Lakis Gigantes.

'She's as ugly as a rotting squid.'

'Why did you marry her then? You could see she was ugly before you married her.'

'Yes but I thought that because she was ugly she would be a virgin.'

'And she was not?'

'No, General.' Lakis Gigantes had been promoted to brigadier general.

'And you really thought that she was so ugly that no man would touch her?'

'Yes.'

'Well, maybe no man touched her.'

'How did she lose her virginity?'

'She could have done this to herself,' said Lakis Gigantes.

'How?'

'Idiot! Do you want me to draw you a picture? Have you asked her?'

'Yes, she swears she has never had another man.'

'Do you have a picture of her?'

'Here, General. That's the only picture that came out. When the photographer tried to take a second one, he fainted.'

'A humorist yet. If I were you, I would believe her. No man but you has touched her. You will never have to worry about being cuckolded and she comes of rich folk. Think about it. You are a sailor. You'll be away a lot. You'll never have to worry about your wife running around. You'll know whose children yours will be.'

'But if the children look like her?'

'You are unlettered. Do you know what Aristotle said? No? Aristotle said,' Lakis Gigantes continued, shamelessly misquoting the philosopher, 'that if a man is very virile, his children will be like him. Now are you or are you not virile?'

The marriage was patched up. There were children who were extremely ugly, as ugly as their father who was the uglier parent of the two.

Along with justice, Lakis Gigantes provided help with rebuilding, hygiene, schooling—the warriors of the Sacred Regiment were put at the disposal of the community practising their peacetime trades as architects, doctors, teachers. When Lakis Gigantes was replaced as Governor, the islanders wept.

Because he was a true Liberal and therefore an opponent of tyrants, of the left or the right, Lakis Gigantes was forced out of the army by IDEA, the secret Fascist organisation which ran the Greek armed forces for the royal family and he was never quite the same. He was born to lead. He had gifts to give but he was not allowed to give. He was not inactive by the standards of other men: he was director general of Greek Broadcasting; he wrote profusely and beautifully: he was elected alderman in Athens and was given the committee chairmanship he wanted, the parks and gardens—he had always planted trees wherever he had gone. And he made sons.

Once, at a mountain resort hotel near Athens, I was calling to my daughters. Two ladies were watching my attempts at parental discipline. They were, surely, Alexandrian ladies, with hennaed hair, much jewellery, speaking the particular mixture of Greek, Arabic, Italian, French and English which one heard only in the prewar salons of the Ptolemaic capital.

'Look how sweet those two little English girls are,' said the first lady.

'Very,' replied the other. 'Isn't it strange how their father resembles Lakis Gigantes. I wonder . . .'

'Don't be absurd, my dear. Lakis Gigantes did not have sons in England,' the first lady retorted.

'Lakis Gigantes had sons everywhere, as you well know,' answered her companion.

144

At a tavern, surrounded by friends, I told father, that evening, about the two Alexandrian ladies. The story was my contribution to the conversation which revolved around the highlights of father's career. The image which emerged from such talk was, like a caricature, incomplete: bold rare lines on the canvas of his life. It was at times like these that I would intervene, breaking the convivial atmosphere by thrusting a major world issue to the fore, asking father harsh, direct questions, demanding answers . . . It's easy to criticise, I would say, but what would you do? Then he would slice to the heart of every matter, analysing clearly, synthesising with ruthless logic, conscious at all times of the possibility of error in what he propounded. And then a hurt look would creep into his eyes, the look of the superb player who is forced to stand on the sidelines. And I would stop asking questions. Conviviality would return: 'tell us general about the time you scared the newspaper editor shitless . . . about the time you took the tramps to the opera . . .' Once, when I walked away early from one of those parties, I finally went home to find that he had been brought back, ill, in a taxi whose driver was undressing him and putting him to bed.

'Thank you,' I said to the driver. 'I'll finish this. You don't have to do it.' I tried to offer a tip and the man was offended:

'Your father, the general, has shed more blood for Greece than any other man. He has held high posts and not a penny of public money stuck to his fingers, unlike others I could name. It is an honour to have looked after him. I shall boast of this to my children.'

And now, in this small flat of his, in London, in 1970, all those many years after his last heroic performance, he was diminished by disease, compelled to caution and wanting to know why I no longer laughed from the heart.

I told him about Mr Han who had said in Korea that I would find the Americans as bad as the Communists.

'Your Mr Han,' said father, 'was wrong. The Americans are not as bad as the Russians. Sure they elected that Johnson but that was by accident and Johnson so disgusted the people that he could not run again and Nixon won because Johnson made it impossible for Humphrey to win. So now they have had two terrible presidents in a row, men of no morality. But then you should not expect too much morality where power lies.'

I told him about Pericles. In disgust after the colonels' coup, I had gone to the University of Toronto in 1967 and immersed myself totally in the glory that was Greece—at least in her golden age—to escape the shame of knowing that Greece was being run in my time by sombre, sanguinary clowns.

'Pericles was an honest politician and a statesman, father. And he won fifteen elections in a row even though he never flattered the people but scolded them when they needed to be scolded.'

'Ah yes,' said father, 'you're quoting Thucydides. Today you could quote the adoring biographers of Kennedy who see only the contrast between Camelot and the filth that followed. Do you know why Pericles won fifteen elections in a row, son? Because things went well for Athens. Sparta was exhausted after fighting her rebelling serfs for ten years and losing the flower of her manhood. Persia was occupied with rebellions in her vast dominions and Athens had no valid rivals for those fifteen years. Pericles gave people jobs, booty from raids on Persian possessions, salaries to serve in the fleet, free tickets to watch the plays of Sophocles. No one was really poor. Everyone was proud to hear Pericles say that Athens was the teacher of Greece. Didn't Harold Ickes explain Roosevelt's successive victories by saying that nobody shoots Santa Claus? It could have been said of Pericles.'

'Couldn't it happen again, father, the golden age?'

'Not in Greece, not now. A golden age has an infrastructure of power. We don't have it now, as Athens had it in the Golden Age. America has it. But I fear she is no Athens, despite her men of genius, her wealth, her skills. I see her more like Sybaris, bound to disappear through over-indulging her appetites. They'll eat and drink their land and the earth barren. Didn't that idiot Lyndon Johnson say that every American's piece of the pie could grow bigger because America's pie will keep getting bigger? And he said that when his astronauts told him, from thousands of miles out, that Earth is a closed-system spaceship which has no way of replenishing its resources. And don't the businessmen love the Johnson doctrine? I was reading in a magazine a slogan "Step up to Chrysler", in other words spend more and more so that more and more raw materials can be used up, more gasoline burned. It won't be fun to be a vassal of the United States.'

He decided to go back to see Greece one more time before he died.

'When I know my time has come,' he said, 'I'll return to London. Cremate me and bury me in my friend George Jellicoe's garden, in Wiltshire, and take my remains back to Greece when the land is free again.'

Next time I saw him was the 10th of October 1970, in a hospital bed. He had flown to London to die. He could not speak. I told him I was there and asked him to squeeze my hand three times if he understood. I felt three feeble squeezes, there was one last smile on his face, and then he died.

I buried him in the quiet Wiltshire garden where he wanted to lie until Greece was free again.

The Greek Ambassador to London, a supporter of the junta, called on me to urge me to take father's remains back to Greece immediately:

'He is the country's greatest hero, the commander of the legendary Sacred Regiment, the third such regiment in our history. He must be buried in the field of Ares, next to the monument of Pelopidas who commanded the first Sacred Regiment which defeated Sparta in ancient times, and next to the monument to Ypsilantis who commanded the second Sacred Regiment that fought for Greek independence under the Turks. Your father belongs to Greece and Greece is more than any of her governments.'

'He did not want to lie in Greece, Mister Ambassador, not until the land was rid of the dictatorship.'

'Your father's heroism and his place in history transcend such things as forms of government.'

I am afraid that at that moment I burst into tears: 'My uncle Yanis' heroism and his place in history transcended forms of government, yet when a right wing government took over after the liberation from the Germans, Yanis Gigantes' name was erased from the signs of the street in which he had fallen fighting for freedom and his bones were dug up from the cemetery where he had been given burial and thrown on a dung heap. And he was as fervently anti-Communist as you.'

'That was the mistake of a minor functionary, doubtlessly.'

'I don't want your minor functionaries sullying my father's grave,' I said. 'I'll wait till civilised men rule Greece again.'

Since then we have had the fuel crisis, wars, famines, a US administration whose members have been convicted and jailed for criminal acts. The US seems to be floundering. Is she the new Sybaris incapable of self-discipline, too addicted to getting an ever larger part of the pie?

When I think of some Americans, I have to answer yes,

Americans like the Senator who said that those US citizens who are mediocre should be represented on the supreme court; the power-hungry men around Nixon; the men who spend millions advertising to make American workers spend more—step up to Chrysler—and then deplore the wage demands of these workers; the blue collar workers who supported George Wallace; the profiteers of oil; the late Senator Kerr and his use of political power to gain wealth; the salacious files of J. Edgar Hoover and the use that was made of them; the ambassadorships for sale; the nearly universal electronic surveillance and its tentacular interconnections with credit bureaus; the mafia and its hold on the economy.

If I were a prisoner of the Communists again, talking to some Mr Han, could I say, as I had said in 1952 that in America, the leader of the West, the inevitable, the necessary, the creative conflict between individuality and order can go on, as it must go on, under enlightened, living law, wise enough to change as life changes? Could I say, if I were a prisoner of the Communists again, that I and other individuals stand a better chance to oppose authority successfully and thereby defend individuality? When I think of Lyndon Johnson's gang, and Nixon's gang, and 'The Selling of the President', I lose heart and say that, at most, I could say to a Communist jailor that I saw no difference between two stifling orders that dominate the world, that the individual doesn't stand a chance anywhere.

But then, I think of other Americans I have known, David Brinkley, honest and great lawyers like W. Crosby Roper and his wife Laura; Tom Lambert, a journalist; Izzy Stone who ran his own weekly to keep the country honest; those who had the courage to solve the Yablonski murder; Peter Lisagor—other journalists; Gordon Wagonet of the Labour Department and his wife Maggie; the young nurses who babysat my children; Judge John Sirica; Elliot Richardson; Averell Harriman; countless honest and conscientious legislators, Mondale, Hubert Humphrey, Eugene McCarthy, General James L. Gavin and above all the great American Press, *The New York Times, The Los Angeles Times, Newsweek, The Washington Post, Time Magazine, The Baltimore Sun, The Chicago Daily News, The Christian Science Monitor, The Louisville Courier Journal, The Milwaukee Journal, The St. Louis Post Dispatch,* CBS News, NBC News, and the rest of the media who fight the good fight. And their men, like Philip Potter, and Clifton Daniel, and Mike Wallace,

148

Walter Cronkite, Eric Sevareid, Mary McGrory, James Reston, Harrison Salisbury, John Osborne, Jack Anderson, the men who write The Bulletin of Atomic Scientists . . . I think of these people, legislators, judges, journalists and countless others, not in categories, but who say the truth, in speech, in writing, in the ballot box. They succeeded, by due process, in exposing criminal acts at the very seat of power, in the White House, to get rid of a corrupt administration without a revolution and then I say to myself that there surely is hope that the US will not become the new Sybaris because too many powerful voices will tell the truth to the American people; that they will not allow the right to individuality to be interpreted, only as the right to seek an ever larger slice of the pie; that they might even change the misinterpretation of the Calvinist ethic which says that material success is a sign that one is the elect of God.

And then, I ask myself whether I can have hope that these good Americans might make it possible for people everywhere to have better government than they now have. And then pessimism floods over me again because the machinery of state has become too large even in smaller countries. Even a Pericles could not control it. It is a power unto itself, this international caste that is called bureaucracy, private or public, and it is strangely similar wherever it may operate. It is a co-optive society where the elders choose successors in their own image and all spend untold energy hiding past failures instead of planning new successes. And because things are getting bigger, more complex, each and all of these bureaucracies are a vast inbred conglomerate of inbred parts which become increasingly more concerned with themselves, spending increasingly more time keeping the people elect from knowing too much. Nowhere did I see this being more true than in Washington where I observed the phenomenon for ten years. But it is true elsewhere.

Can then the truth-sayers prevail over the seekers after bigger slices of pie and the careful writers of defensive memoranda?

I ask the question and I fear to answer it. But I have found that there is one place where I need not fear the answers. I discovered it when I decided to take a child to a circus. I hoped, through the child, to remember sweet things long past. The child, Eve-Marie, was shy, even suspicious, because I was a sudden intruder in her life, an intruder who menaced, maybe, the order of her world. But she could not resist the circus. She ate cotton candy, hugged a toy dog and gravely watched the clowns. She spoke no words, but when it was over she held my hand and looked deceived when another small girl crawled onto my knee. It took months before she said she loved me—loved me, not because of all the things I might have been, not because of my unaccomplished missions, but because I could turn her into a trombone, or a banjo, and made her believe that she could be an oboe. She loved me also because of the lady with the green hair who—I said—had a tumultuous life, what with humming-birds mistaking her for a tree when she stood up and goats thinking she was grass when she lay down.

In Eve-Marie's home, my father's sword, which now hangs there, is not a reproach for what I have not done. For Eve-Marie's mother, Sylvie, friendship is not the prelude to reproach; acceptance is not unthinkable; companionship is not a combat.

And I have my older daughters to whom I can express my love, Eleni and Claire, my brother, my mother, my friends.

Pericles would have called me an 'idiotes', a private man. He meant that as an insult and it is the origin of our word 'idiot'. I am not sure Pericles would have thought it wrong to be an 'idiotes' in our present age.

THE SUPPORTING EVIDENCE

In the preceding pages, I accused the Greek dictatorial regime of brutality and corruption; I said that though the Americans knew of this brutality and corruption, they supported the dictatorial regime; I made serious charges about the family of the former Greek monarch, Constantine, during the First World War; I discussed the US role in the 1974 invasion of Cyprus by Turkey. The charges I made are serious: that is why I supply evidence, in the form of three appendices A, B and C containing extracts from documents published by:

(A)   The Council of Europe
(B)   and (C) by the US House of Representatives.

A fourth appendix, D, gives the reference numbers of documents published by the German Foreign Office on its dealings with the former Greek Royal Family in the First World War.

CONSULTATIVE ASSEMBLY OF THE COUNCIL OF EUROPE

24 April 1972   Doc. 3114

REPORT
on the situation in Greece
(Rapporteur : Mr. DANKERT)

I. DRAFT RESOLUTION
presented by the Committee
on European Non-Member Countries[2]

The Assembly,

1. Recalling its Recommendations 511 (1968) and 547 (1969) concerning the situation in Greece;

2. Deploring that, despite promises to the contrary, five years after the coup d'état of 21 April 1967 Greece is still not on its way to the restoration of parliamentary democratic government;

3. Noting that martial law has only been very partially abolished and that Greek citizens are today still deprived of their civil rights;

4. Condemning the continued violation of individual human rights by the regime in Athens,

5. Invites its members to urge their governments to exert all their influence to :

  (a) enable impartial observers to be given adequate facilities to enquire into the treatment of prisoners in Greece and to collect information on alleged practices of torture in Greek prisons and police offices;

(b) stop the arbitrary arrests and the detention without trial of Greek citizens under the control of the regime in Athens;

(c) procure the abolition of martial law in all districts of Greece;

6. Further invites its members to press their governments to use their influence, either individually or collectively, with the object of allowing the Greek people freely to express their will as to the nature of their regime and government;

7. Expresses the hope that the conditions may soon come about that will enable the Members of the Council of Europe to welcome Greece once more in the community of European democratic nations;

8. Directs its Committee on European Non-Member Countries to continue to follow the situation in Greece.

II. EXPLANATORY MEMORANDUM
by Mr. DANKERT

... The opposition to the regime kept manifesting itself in a number of declarations, one of them made on the occasion of the 150th anniversary of Greek independence, on 25 May. A group of 133 leading figures from the field of journalism and the arts signed a manifesto calling for the restoration of sovereignty and human rights for the people of Greece. It denied the right of any single group to claim a 'monopoly of patriotism' or to 'act as the authentic interpreter of the nation's will'. It said: 'The nation has no will distinct from that of our people, expressed according to the rule of the majority and through freely elected representatives.' One of the signatories was Mr George Seferis, the Nobel prize-winner, who said: 'The suspension of the people's sovereignty and of human rights arrests the fruitful flow of national life, opens the way to other constitutional deviations, deprives the country of the normal renewal of its political forces, and leads it to spiritual and political withering. It also means that a considerable number of Greeks— many among them distinguished for their services to the country and its allies—find themselves in prison or in deportation either for their beliefs alone or for acts inspired by their devotion to freedom. It is a national imperative that this state of affairs should be ended without delay.'

Torture and prison conditions

... One ... defendant, Mr Constantine Kostarakos, repeated the account of the tortures he had undergone, at his trial before the Athens Criminal (i.e. non-military) Court on 3 August. The court rose briefly after Mr Kostarakos's mother, who was present, had fainted on hearing her son's account, and on resuming the Chairman of the court refused to allow the defendant to give any further details about the tortures he had suffered. In the recent trial of 8 members of the Panhellenic Liberation Movement (PAK), who were tried for a bomb plot by the Military Court in Athens on 20 and 21 January 1972, the defendants Kyriasis, Valyrakis, Kyrijios and Spiliopoulos declared that they had been tortured. Kyriasis also mentioned police officer Haralambos, who acted as a witness for the prosecution. With regard to Haralambos, Kyriasis said during the trial: 'The witness lied when he said I wanted to play the hero. I am sorry. He remembered very well, however, that he beat me on the soles of the feet with an iron bar, while others beat me on the chest.' . . .

Complaints have also been made about conditions in both the internment camps . . . and in prisons . . . detainees were deported or interned in primitive gaols, some of them being kept in solitary confinement for a year at a time . . . The complaints about prison conditions indicate that there is a connection between the worsening of those conditions and the decision of the Greek Government to terminate the agreement with the International Red Cross on the inspection of the detention centres.

At the same time the number of political prisoners continued to increase as fresh charges were made and sentences passed, often apparently regardless of the provisions of the regime's own constitution. The large group of people arrested in November 1970 were not charged until the following May, although they were kept in detention in the meanwhile . . . Mr George Romaios editor of the newspaper *Vima*, was arrested by military police, without any reason being given; Professor Demetrius Maronilis, a dismissed lecturer at Salonika University, was arrested presumably because he had contributed to an anthology of anti-totalitarian prose . . .

Although the regime had repeatedly said that the group of people arrested after 28 November 1970 were accused of sedition (which now fell within the competence of civilian courts), six of them, including Mr Sartzetakis,* the former judge, were faced with charges involving conspiracy and explosives, thus remaining within the jurisdiction of the military courts. The accused were allowed to see their lawyers for the first time since their arrest six months previously, and Mr Sartzetakis was finally released on 19 November

* (Note by Philip Deane: Mr Sartzetakis was the prosecutor who inculpated police officers in the murder of Gregory Lambrakis, the case described in the film 'Z'. Mr Sartzetakis has testified that he was tortured for eleven months.)

1971 . . . Furthermore, the partial transfer of jurisdiction from military to civilian courts has not brought any decrease in the number of political arrests . . .

The US Government, in spite of congressional criticism, continued its policy of support for the Greek regime. Mr David Packard, at that time Deputy Defence Secretary, visited Athens in May 1971 and was reported to have returned with a list of Greek military requirements. In July a State Department official, speaking before a House of Representatives sub-committee, rejected the idea of cutting US military aid to Greece as a means of persuading the government to adopt more liberal policies . . .

In declarations he made during a visit to Greece in October, Vice-President Agnew seemed to go beyond this line of policy in expressing his support for the Greek regime. Mr Agnew said, in his farewell message : 'I leave with renewed respect for the efforts of the Government of Greece in carrying out its country's role as a Member of NATO' but omitted the customary call for progress towards a return to democracy. At the end of February 1972 Congress voted to cut off military aid to Greece, but included a saving clause which allowed the President to restore it, provided he certified that 'the overriding requirements of the national security' so dictated. This the President had done 17 February, and the appropriate Congress committees were so informed on 2 March. His decision was sharply attacked by Senator Edmund Muskie (Democrat, Maine) who said that to resume military aid to Greece was 'immoral' and a 'waste' of US military assistance. Already at the beginning of February an agreement was announced between the US and Greek navies which provided that the port of Piraeus should be used as a base for the US Sixth Fleet. It is estimated that as a result of this agreement an additional 9500 US citizens— officers, men and their families—will be stationed in Greece, spending some $150 million a year in the country. There have recently been reports that a 50% increase in US military aid to Greece was to be requested, and that the Greek Government was considering the purchase of 'Phantom' aircraft.

Relations with Western European countries

Mr Jean de Lipkowski, French Secretary of State for Foreign Affairs, paid an official visit to Greece from 27 to 29 January 1972, the first West European Minister to do so since the coup d'état in 1967. During his visit, Mr de Lipkowski said that 'France and Greece have always been on the same side, because they have always struggled for the cause of freedom', although he also pointed out that 'the present conception of democracy in Greece and France was not the same'. The Secretary of State said that Paris would try to improve relations between Athens and the Common Market countries, and would, if necessary, contribute to Greece's military security. Mr de Lipkowski was not, he said, an arms-dealer, but it is known that the Greek Government has studied the possibility of buying Mirage aircraft. France has other important commercial interests in Greece, whose second largest foreign trade partner she is, and French firms are hoping to share in some large commercial projects. Meanwhile, it was announced at the end of 1971 that the Government of the Federal Republic of Germany intended, as a Member of NATO, to supply Greece with some military aid in the following year. This was separate from the private order for submarines which the Greek Government had placed with a Kiel shipbuilding firm, four years previously . . .

Even if some sharp attacks on her domestic policies have been made by member governments, more often outside than inside the NATO Ministerial Council, the increased strategic importance of the Eastern Mediterranean has enabled Greece to maintain its position in the Alliance. The uncertainties about future developments concerning Yugoslavia may strengthen this position even further. The most outspoken critics of Greece's domestic policy have been Denmark and Norway. In addressing the NATO Assembly in Ottawa, Canada's Foreign Minister was also highly critical and the NATO Assembly itself condemned any repression of democratic freedoms in Greece as 'dangerous to the internal cohesion of NATO' and called on 'the government in Athens to undertake immediately serious steps leading to the restoration of democratic freedoms' . . .

What conclusions should be drawn from the events of the last fifteen months in Greece? . . .

In the field of human rights the Council of Europe has a special task. The ideals of this organisation till 1967 were also the ideals of Greece. Representatives of the Greek people, serving in the Committee of Ministers and in the Consultative Assembly, have defended them as we do. Our solidarity with those freely elected former representatives of the Greek people should lead us to a more strict attitude on the state of human rights in Greece than in countries which never knew freely elected representatives . . . Greeks are still being put on trial for expressing their political opposition to the government by the only means available to them, whether before the military or civilian courts. There has been delay in bringing people to trial and defence lawyers have been prevented from communicating with their clients, sometimes for months at a time. There have been allegations of torture from different and reliable sources. In view of the Greek authorities' previous record in this matter together with the impossibility, particularly since the end of the ICRC's agreement with the Greek Government, of these allegations being either refuted or confirmed by an impartial enquiry, we have to treat them as overwhelming prima facie evidence of torture demanding an impartial enquiry. There can scarcely be any doubt that the violation of basic human rights is the legitimate concern of the Council of Europe. The Consultative Assembly should remain uncompromising in this field.

EXTRACTS FROM THE REPORT OF A STUDY MISSION TO GREECE JANUARY 18 TO 21, 1974

FEBRUARY 1974

Printed for the use of the Committee on Foreign Affairs

Letter of Transmittal

Washington, D.C., February 22, 1974.

Hon. Thomas E. Morgan,
Chairman, Committee on Foreign Affairs, US House of Representatives, Washington, DC.

Dear Mr Chairman : I enclose a report of the special study mission to Greece which I conducted from January 18-21, 1974, accompanied by Clifford Hackett, staff consultant to the Subcommittee on Europe.

We have tried, in these pages, to analyze the problems facing the Greek people today. Since these problems also affect long-established American interests in that country, we have tried to indicate the possible consequences of the present political and economic chaos in Greece for our country.

We have not, however, tried to cover every aspect of the present Greek situation. Past shortcomings of American policy have not been detailed. Instead we concentrate on present problems and options.

We hope this report will be useful to Members of Congress and to all persons concerned about US relations to Greece and to Europe. We have included in the appendix a report on the situation in Greece prepared for the recent meeting of the Council of Europe's Consultative Assembly which was attended by a delegation of the committee which it was my honour to lead. This excellent report, by Mr Victor Abens of Luxembourg, illustrates well the European concern for the situation in Greece.

Your comments and those of any of our colleagues on the full committee will be most welcome.

Respectfully submitted,

Donald M. Frazer,
Chairman, Subcommittee on International
Organisations and Movements.

Summary and Conclusions

The conclusions from this study mission to Athens, and the recommendations for changes in US policy toward Greece, are based on over 40 interviews during January 1974 with Greek political leaders, officials of the American Embassy, a minister in the present Greek Government and with many private Greek citizens. Names and other identifying information have been omitted from the report to protect the confidence with which these conversations were conducted.

We should note, however, that the broadest possible range of interviews was sought. We spoke to former ministers of the earlier parliamentary governments; to present leaders of the identifiable political groups in Greece from the conservative to the radical; to members of resistance groups; to Greek businessmen; and to students. We visited the homeporting sites of our Navy. We spoke to a former political prisoner and army officer whose tortures at the hands of the Greek military police have left him paralyzed and speechless. We spoke with those who have fled from Greece during the military dictatorship and to those who sought to destroy that dictatorship through violence.

The following pages attempt to summarize the political events leading to the extremely serious situation which today exists in Greece. Part of the report is a summary of pre-1967 events which we include to aid the reader in assessing the present options in Greece for that country and for our own.

Conclusions

(1) Our principal conclusion, on the situation in Greece, is that the present government cannot long endure. Marked by inexperience, its members appear without the requisite talents or skills for extricating the country from its political and economic chaos. The important question is by whom and how this extrication will take place.

(2) The second conclusion is that the democratic opposition in Greece is united as never before while the government is divided among three or four groups each attempting to influence the present de facto leader, Gen. Dimitrios Ioannides. How the

160

democratic opposition can influence Ioannides to find a peaceful and secure exit from present dead-end is the principal political question in Greece today.

(3) For the United States, the principal conclusion from our report is that we have pursued a faulty policy since 1967 from which we must now extricate ourselves. There is no easy way to do this. Damage has already occurred to American interests in Greece and more will occur before the present situation ends. To redeem US interests and terminate an unfortunate appearance of support for authoritarian rule, we recommend the following actions:

Recommendations

(A) A public announcement that the US aircraft carrier scheduled to homeport in Greece this summer will not be deployed under existing circumstances, and that we are awaiting unequivocal and irreversible steps toward a free electoral process which will end military rule.

(B) The assignment of a new American ambassador who comes free of identification with past American policies, either with their design in Washington or their execution in Greece. This is said without regard to any criticism of the present ambassador or his predecessors, or their staffs, or of the present authors of American policy toward Greece in Washington. A fresh start is needed by a seasoned political observer who can understand the present events in Greece and advise the President on their consequences for the United States.

No one can be certain that these actions will help the citizens of Greece regain control over their own destinies. But America's responsibility to its own traditions and our enlightened self-interest coincide, we believe, in mandating these two steps as the minimum response to today's Greece. They will also indicate a shift toward solidarity with our European NATO allies in their more consistent opposition to the Greek dictatorship.

Inactivity may be the principal hazard which Washington, preoccupied elsewhere, must overcome unless Greece is to become a major problem for the United States in their near future. For Greece, but also for the United States, the present dangers are great and the time is short.

The Background

Until April, 1967, Greece was governed by a parliamentary democracy under a constitutional monarchy. The widespread impression that Greece had a highly unstable government since the Civil War (1946-49) is historically inaccurate . . .

161

The period of 1949 to 1952 saw a somewhat unstable condition in that many different governments ruled in this period. But these rapid changes were more apparent than real or significant. Many of the same parliamentary leaders participated in these governments. The quality of civil government and administration, while modest, was relatively undisturbed by these frequent changes of political leaders.

From 1955 to 1963, the conservative government under Constantine Karamanlis ruled Greece in an unusual period of political stability . . .

The 'Crisis Years'

The 'crisis years' of the 1960's began with the disputed outcome of the October 1961 election which maintained Karamanlis and his party (ERE-National Radical Union) in power. The newly-formed Centre Union Party (a loose and centrifugal coalition of moderate Liberal/Conservative forces under the aegis of veteran politicians George Papandreou and Sophocles Venizelos) denounced the 1961 elections as fraudulent and accused Karamanlis of subverting the popular will in collaboration with the Greek Army and Gendarmerie.

Following nearly 2 years of relentless political pounding by the opposition, the highly emotional aftermath of the assassination of Greek leftist deputy Gregory Lambrakis, in Thessaloniki, and a shrouded but bitter controversy with King Paul and Queen Frederika, Karamanlis resigned in the summer of 1963 and called for new elections in 45 days.

The Royal House, at that time, became involved in a series of intricate political manoeuvres (e.g. the naming of two interim governments under Pipinelis and Mavromichalis rather than proceeding with elections) obviously designed to weaken Karamanlis. These manoeuvres undoubtedly contributed to the squeezing of Karamanlis not only out of power but also out of the leadership of his political party—ERE. He was succeeded by Panayotis Kanellopoulos.

The November 1963 elections gave a plurality but not a majority in Parliament to the George Papandreou forces. It took another election in February of 1964 to bring the Centre Union in firm control of the country with a landslide (53 per cent of the popular vote and over three-fifths of the deputies in Parliament).

The transition from Conservative to Liberal Centre Union rule took place quite peacefully—but it should be noted that royal manoeuvres contributed heavily to the political demise of Karamanlis as well as continued a dangerous (potentially polarizing) precedent of royal involvement in politics.

162

After less than 18 months in power, a head-on collision-course was structured by a politically-animated environment and pitted young King Constantine against ageing George Papandreou. The major substantive disagreement seemed to be over the issue of who would retain control of the Greek Armed Forces. Would it be the hereditary but constitutional monarch or would it be the elected Prime Minister? Constantine soon manoeuvred George Papandreou into resigning (July 1965).

Then he continued to cultivate existing divisions in the leadership of the Centre Union by refusing to call new elections and by asking minority faction Centre Union deputies (e.g. S. Stephanopoulos and C. Mitsotakis) to form a shaky government with ERE support.

King Constantine's subsequent manoeuvres which strained the letter as well as the spirit of the Greek Constitution, gave rise to massive popular demonstrations in Athens and Thessaloniki. The people felt that the popular will was being subverted. A mood of impending constitutional crisis was further cultivated by a hyperactive and bitterly divided press.

The Crisis On Cyprus

This crisis was taking place against a backdrop of imminent war between Greece and Turkey over the disposition of the island of Cyprus. The Cyprus issue which had, once more, flared up in December 1963 threatened to disrupt NATO unity in the Eastern Mediterranean. The United States, despite an official policy of neutrality and nonintervention in Greece's domestic affairs, appears to have sided, throughout 1965-67, with King Constantine (and the Conservative forces which had coalesced around him) and against George Papandreou. Apparently the Conservatives were expected to take a more moderate (i.e. pro-NATO) line vis-à-vis Turkey on the subject of Cyprus.

Another important reason for the pro-Conservative US policies (which have proven fundamentally unwise and short-sighted ex-post-facto) might have been the extreme sensitivity of US representatives in Athens to Andreas Papandreou. This American educated economist, son of the late George Papandreou, emerged as the leader of a vocal and abrasive faction in the Centre Union Party. Andreas demanded less US intervention in domestic Greek affairs and a thorough overhaul of what he considered an ailing and corrupt Greek political system. His chances of coming to power, after George Papandreou's death, were excellent.

Despite the atmosphere of tension and crisis in the political superstructure of the country (1965 to 1967), the economic and social infractructures continued to grow vigorously, apparently undis-

163

turbed by 'political instability'. For example, in the economy, GNP yearly growth rates continued at the extremely effective 8 per cent range, while the political demonstrations were by comparative standards quite restrained—one accidental death in 1965. Finally, in the cultural and educational sectors Greece was experiencing rapid transformation and growth.

Even the imperfect political system provided a peaceful way out of the crisis. Following an agreement among the major protagonists of the Greek political drama (Constantine, G. Papandreou and Kanellopoulos) general elections were set for May 27, 1967. The electoral outcome would have probably brought George Papandreou (and the Centre Union) back to the controls with a solid majority. But, out of the long-standing secret and paramilitary organisations, within the military establishment came the Papadopoulos April 21, 1967 coup d'état. Thus, the Greek people were forcibly prevented from exercising their right to self-government.

Since April 21, 1967

The political developments since the Papadopoulos coup have been fragmented, erratic and ultimately ineffectual. Whether or not the junta leader intended a true liberalisation (if so, he would have been the first European dictator to step down voluntarily), the regime's attempts to deal with political society were inept . . .

The decision of the chief of the military police, General Ioannides, to replace Papadopoulos in the coup of November 25, 1973 was based initially on some or all of these elements :

(1) The apparent inability of Papadopoulos to handle the student demonstrations effectively.

(2) The personal power aggrandisement of Papadopoulos as evidenced by the ending of the monarchy and his assumption of the Presidency for an 8-year term with enhanced powers.

(3) The corruption within the Papadopoulos government. (This was apparently personally obnoxious to Ioannides whose bitterest opponents admit his scrupulous honesty and incorruptibility.)

(4) Indications that the economy was out of control. Aside from Ioannides himself, and whatever small group of army officers who followed his directions in executing the November 25 coup, no one seems to know precisely which of these four elements, or which combination of them, precipitated the coup.

Ioannides has remained obscure in his military police office, apparently unchanged in his working habits since November 25. Papadopoulos and some close associates were placed under house arrest, but otherwise were unharmed.

164

The real truth of Ioannides' intentions may only slowly unfold in the coming months but observers in Greece today give him only a limited time to make some key decisions. The obscure and inexperienced people chosen by Ioannides for the present cabinet indicate that it must be seen as a temporary government, whether or not that was Ioannides' intention . . .

A . . . group of officers who could influence Ioannides are his fellow military police officers who are personally loyal to him and who, presumably, are responsible for the tortures and other severe forms of political repression evident during the past 7 years . . .

There is complacency among official Americans about what a postdictatorship Greece will mean for the United States. 'Where else can the Greeks go?' is a frequent rejoinder to the fear that the rising level of anti-American sentiment will carry over into the new democratic Greece.

The deep roots of Greek anti-Communism, nurtured by the tragic civil war which most adults still remember, remain a strong force in Greek society. The close ties to NATO within the Greek armed forces are still a reality, though it has been diminished to an undetermined extent by purges of the officer corps by the two dictators.

But no country can endure 7 years of police state rule without some repercussions. The apathy of its European allies in both NATO and the European Community have weakened Greece's ties to the West. The fact that the United States continued to press, in the name of NATO, its naval and air base rights during the dictatorship, make our country more culpable in the eyes of many Greeks than are the European countries of NATO which are still dominated by American strategic thinking . . .

The role of the United States in post-1967 Greece is a classic example of the consequences of military predominance in American foreign policy. Having operated for nearly 7 years on the premise that vital US military interests demand 'getting along' with the Greek military government, we find it difficult to assert a primacy of political interests . . . This difficulty consists of an admission that US policy in Greece since 1967 has been in essential error. Governments find such admissions painful . . .

When events forced a choice between either ignoring political developments like the illegal seizure of power in Greece in April, 1967 or risking a loss of our military presence, the military side won. The same military interests predominating in our European policies are demonstrated in the unfortunate efforts by the United States to add another authoritarian government to NATO, the country of Spain . . .

CYPRUS—1974

EXTRACTS FROM HEARINGS
before the
COMMITTEE ON FOREIGN AFFAIRS
and its
SUB-COMMITTEE ON EUROPE
HOUSE OF REPRESENTATIVES
NINETY-THIRD CONGRESS
second session
August 19 and 20, 1974

Preface
The role of the United States in the world today, and in the future, will not allow a false choice of domestic versus international concerns. What we are at home does, and should, affect our foreign policies; and what we do abroad will, and should affect our domestic tranquility and fortunes.

To begin this study in 1974, where these hearings begin, is to start in the middle of a longer and unhappy story of American-Greek relations since 1967. In that year a military junta seized power in Athens and thereby provided a unique test for both the United States and the NATO alliance to which both countries belong. In the 25 years of the alliance there has never been another case like Greece where a functioning democracy was turned into a dictatorship.

The initial American reaction to that event was hesitation, followed gradually by the establishment of 'normal' relations with the dictatorship. But a ban on the shipment of major US military aid items imposed in April 1967 by the Johnson administration remained in effect for the Nixon administration to evaluate in 1969. A resolution came late in the year with the decision to remove that ban in 1970. This was apparently decided when the new US Ambassador, Henry Tasca, arrived in Athens in January 1970. The following September the ban was rescinded with a curious announcement about improving the Greek ability to strengthen the NATO southern flank, coupled with a comment that a 'trend toward a constitutional order (in Greece) is established.'

Of course, no such trend was evident nor in existence. The Papadopoulos dictatorship took Greece on a downward spiral which ultimately brought the country (and the dictator himself) to the brink of disaster in November 1973. A new and even more oppressive dictatorship followed under General Dimitrios Ioannides which was as disastrous as it was short-lived. It was General Ioannides who led Greece, and the United States, into the tragic involvement in Cyprus which these pages describe.

Why did the United States persist in its tacit support for dictatorial government in Greece? Why, in the crucial week of July 15, 1974 . . . did not the United States publicly demand a reversal of acts by the Greek dictatorship which clearly produced a disaster bound to involve our country?

The answer to these questions is found, I believe, in the 4 years of hearings and reports which the Sub-Committee on Europe has produced in its examination of American policies toward Greece. The bitter summary conclusion these many pages yield is that the United States chose to ignore the fate of democracy in Greece in order to maintain its military base rights in that country.

Both a Democratic and a Republican administration share the responsibilities for this policy since the same concept of a priority of military considerations over political development animated American policy toward Greece from before 1967 to the present. But the last 5 years, which include the restoration of full aid to the Greek dictatorship, and the persistent refusal to criticise that regime, are obviously more clearly related to the present crisis in Cyprus.

During these 5 years our country abused both Greek hospitality and our own responsibilities to democratic government by tolerating a military junta in Athens as long as it provided us with air and naval bases. When the junta provoked a coup on Cyprus against that republic's legal government, we ignored the affront, hoping that the world (and Turkey) would accept another dictatorship without protest . . .

The lesson of American policy toward Greece, of which Cyprus is a part, is not a matter for diplomatic historians only. There will be occasions in Europe and elsewhere in the coming months and years where the United States must choose between stability and change, between short-term military advantages and long-term political development and between a comfortable liaison with alliances of the past and more difficult choices in dealing with new leaders and new forces of the future. Portugal, Spain, and Italy are only the most obvious possibilities in Europe where these dilemmas may arise.

How our country responds and, therefore, how our leaders understand these choices, will become, I believe, a major foreign policy question for our country.

Benjamin S. Rosenthal,

November 28, 1974.   Chairman, Sub-Committee on Europe.

CYPRUS—1974

Monday, August 19, 1974.

House of Representatives,
Committee on Foreign Affairs,
Sub-Committee on Europe,
Washington, D.C.

The sub-committee met at 11:10 a.m. in room 2172, Rayburn House Office Building, Hon. Benjamin S. Rosenthal (chairman of the sub-committee) presiding.

Past Congressional Concern

Mr Rosenthal :

The Congress has shown considerable concern over the past 7 years for American policy in Greece since that country fell under a military dictatorship. That concern was centred on whether, and how, the United States should disengage itself from a government that was increasingly repressive and which repudiated everything which the NATO alliance of democracies was supposed to represent.

It was, therefore, a problem of direct American interest when the junta in Athens was itself overthrown last November and replaced by an even more repressive dictatorship. A report by this committee in January foresaw an early end to that second-generation junta.

The end came with a military adventure on Cyprus which had, as its only beneficial result, the restoration of civilian rule in Athens. But the circumstances of that restoration indicate a tragedy for all principals, including the United States, of dimensions that are not yet known or perhaps even established.

There is no doubt that Greece holds the United States directly responsible for these events both for sins of commission and of

168

omission. The bonds between our country and Greece are jeopardized today by this bitter judgment of a close and traditional ally. Equally grave, the enmity between Greece and Turkey precipitated by the Cyprus crisis will endure for years and perhaps decades . . .

Mr Sarbanes. Now, I would assume that, as a professional diplomat, you would not expect a conference (the Geneva peace talks on Cyprus) of the sort that was convened in Geneva to produce instant results would you?

Mr Hartman (US Assistant Secretary of State for European Affairs). No, that is correct.

Mr Sarbanes. Now, the talks broke down at a time when Foreign Secretary Callaghan had requested another 36 hours—of course there is no guarantee that 36 hours would have produced a result, but that is what they asked for for consultation. The Foreign Secretary termed the refusal of Turkey to accede to that request arbitrary and unreasonable. . . . On Tuesday, the 13th of August, the State Department issued a statement on Cyprus setting forth the US position, which included recognition of the status of the Turkish community on Cyprus as requiring improvement and protection, a greater degree of autonomy . . . Of course according to press reports that statement has been interpreted by some diplomats, 'in the day's context those were the magic words Turkey had been waiting for,' in other words as constituting an American underwrite of the Turkish position. And I only note that at 5 o'clock on the morning following issuance of the statement Turkish forces struck at Nicosia and in the direction of Famagusta . . .

Ecevit, on Thursday, August 15, after meeting with Ambassador Macomber, told reporters that Turkey is very happy with the frank and open US policy on Cyprus. Again at a press conference in Ankara the following day, just on Friday, he said he had had frequent telephone conversations with Secretary of State Kissinger and he strongly praised the American role.

He said that Washington had been less emotional and more objective than Britain, whose Foreign Secretary Callaghan denounced Turkey for breaking off the Geneva talks.

The United States, Ecevit said, had evaluated the problem objectively, refrained from taking sides, refrained from pressures.

Did you assume that when Turkey reached the Attila line that its forward movement of armed forces would stop?

169

Mr Hartman. We were assured by the Turkish Prime Minister that that was in fact their intention.

Mr Sarbanes. That has not happened.

Mr Hartman. That has not happened . . .

Mr Sarbanes. Is it the Department's position, as I understand from your testimony this morning, that you intend to leave it to the two communities to work out a constitutional settlement? When you say the two communities I take it you mean the Turkish Cypriot community and the Greek Cypriot community; is that correct?

Mr Hartman. They should be ultimately responsible for agreeing on what the constitutional situation should be on the island.

Mr Sarbanes. How do you propose that that be worked out in any fair basis when there are 40,000 Turkish troops on the island of Cyprus who even at this moment are continuing to engage in armed conflict and to expand their territorial control on that island? . . .

Mr Kyros (addressing Mr Hartman). A few questions. The thing that bothers me most as I listened to you this morning, and I have a lot of respect for you, even though I may have different judgments, is that somehow you seem to talk as if we have dealt even-handedly in Cyprus. We simply have not. A Turkish marauding force of 30,000 to 40,000, armed with M-60 machine-guns, Sky-hawks, our landing craft, our helmets, our bullets, our ships, has been violating our basic agreement. We only give these weapons to nations for defensive purposes under the NATO agreement we made.

We have been sitting on the Greeks in effect since they began this military misadventure through their junta. But the government is not the same there at all.

What I fail to see—and I discussed this with Mr Kissinger the other day—is why our Nation has not realised that we are standing in front of the world saying we are supplying these weapons to the Turkish Army with whom we would like to have good relations, but they are out there marauding and killing now. They don't have to stop either. There is no reason for them to stop. Some blind Cypriot will fire and the Turks will keep on killing. This will lead to killing by Greek Cypriots in cantons where they hold Turks hostage.

Many of us foresaw this, and that is why it was incumbent on this

Nation not to say we are going to play our cards on down the road, but to tell a nation to whom we supply every last bullet, and every last piece of equipment, 'You must desist or we will stop military and economic aid, and do other things.'

To have the Greeks and Turks at each other's throats is something we have unintentionally assisted in, because we did not act firmly. We were not evenhanded. There is not a Greek national force any longer in Cyprus. How could you and still today permit 30,000 or 40,000 Turkish troops at gunpoint to dictate what is going to happen in Cyprus? . . . .

I already said at the outset that I thought the initial military mis-adventure by the Greek junta was tremendously erroneous, and a grotesquely irrational step. But subsequently, you keep on talking as if it is evenhanded. The Turks have now got that small country at gunpoint. They have the Greek nation at gunpoint, but the idea they would be able to dictate to us with our own weapons is what I would worry about it; we have this unbelievable, uncivilised spectacle of people being displaced and murdered. If you are a hapless peasant against the heavy American weaponry, you are being murdered. There is no other way to talk about it. This is barbarism.

It seems to me, our country, for its own national security, and because it stands for decency, can no longer talk about wrong judgments. You should act, and you should turn your attention to Turkey and begin to call for the withdrawal of all Turkish regular forces and turning the Cypriot country over to a strong United Nations' peacekeeping force . . .

> Tuesday, August 20, 1974
> House of Representatives,
> Committee on Foreign Affairs,
> Sub-Committee on Europe,
> Washington, D.C.

The sub-committee met at 2 p.m., in room 2172, Rayburn House Office Building, Hon. Benjamin S. Rosenthal (chairman of the sub-committee) presiding.

Mr Rosenthal. We are particularly honoured and pleased this afternoon to be joined by the Honourable George Ball, former Under Secretary of State, who served with great distinction in the US Government and has great interest and expertise, knowledge and background in the area under consideration . . .

Mr Ball. Thank you very much, Mr Chairman. I apologise to the committee for not having a prepared statement, but since I only spoke to you last evening, I haven't had an opportunity to prepare one . . . In June of 1964 the US Government received clear intelligence information that there was to be a Turkish invasion the next day. So, that night, Secretary Rusk and I . . . composed a . . . note to the Government in Ankara.

It was, I will admit, a very harsh note to send an ally because it said in effect that the Turkish Government had obligations to the United States in view of all the help the United States had given which this action would violate; that the action would be in violation of the London-Zurich accords which, while they permitted intervention by one of the guarantor powers, permitted that intervention only after consultation with the others and only for the purpose of restoring the status quo that existed at the time that the accords were signed; that it would be in violation of the NATO commitments which Turkey had made; finally, that it would be in violation of the understandings under which the United States had provided military assistance to Turkey with the implication that military assistance would be withdrawn if Turkey persisted in this intention to invade Cyprus. I do not recall now whether it was explicitly stated or not, but this meant not only future military equipment but in effect it also meant the military equipment that had already been provided since such equipment would be useless without a continuing supply of spare parts.

Mr Rosenthal. What was the presumed Turkish motivation for the potential military action?

Mr Ball. The Turks had provocation. In fact, they had considerable in the sense that the Turkish minority was being very badly treated on the island. By that time Cyprus had become an armed camp and a number of people were being killed. When I was there in December 1963, there was already what I think was called the Blue Line, which meant that the city of Nicosia, for example, was divided by barbed wire and that in effect there was a wall separating the Turkish and Greek communities.

There was no doubt at that time that there had been a lot of bloodshed and, in all candour to this commitee, I think Archbishop Makarios was not too concerned about its continuance. So the Turks had a right to be concerned about the situation in the island, but they didn't have a right to invade, particularly unilaterally and without consultation.

One gets into a problem in international law trying to justify it. The Turks, if they tried to justify it at all, did so, I suppose, under article 51 of the United Nations Chapter as an act of self-defence. They were defending other Turks—the Turkish community in the island. They were never explicit about it, but they talked in terms of self-defence and I suppose this is what they had in mind.

Again, they paid no attention to the United Nations and paid no attention to the other guarantor powers. They paid no attention to their obligations under NATO. We hadn't given them all this equipment to use against a common enemy. They paid no attention to the kinds of obligations that they had under the London-Zurich agreements. There was ample justification for this strong note.

I may say this left bruised feelings in Ankara. I know it very well because the night I sent the note I was uncertain as to whether I should cancel an appointment with General de Gaulle in Paris the following day, but one did not cancel an appointment with him lightly, as you may recall.

After I had met with President de Gaulle, I went on to Ankara to see Prime Minister Inonu and discussed the situation at great length with him explaining the American motivations. While he made it clear that the Turkish Government was very upset by the extent of this note, it did work and, although he wouldn't admit it—couldn't admit it, obviously—I think Prime Minister Inonu understood that the United States felt it was essential that this invasion be stopped.

This left its scars, I am sure. On the other hand, I do not at all accept the suggestion now being made to apologise for the present situation, that the strength of this note so damaged our relations with Turkey that we were unable to act effectively in the present crisis. That seems to me to be a disingenuous explanation, if I may say so.

Mr Rosenthal. What do you think would have happened had you not sent the note?

Mr Ball. There would have been an invasion. There wasn't the slightest doubt about it. We had to stop the invasion as we saw it at that time, because, once there was an invasion, then the situation would be totally out of hand. Once the Turks were on the island, it would be very difficult ever to persuade them to leave and we saw no future stability in the situation if the invasion once occurred.

Mr Rosenthal : In your judgment—the fact that the invasion was stopped, did that leave the implication or the conclusion that the United States did have sufficient leverage with the Turks to achieve that objective?

Mr Ball. Well, we had it at that time and we achieved it. All I am suggesting is that the Turks are reasonable people and they saw the realities of the situation, that we were the principal contributor of military support to them, that they were a part of NATO, that we did share a common enemy, or antagonist, or whatever you want to call it, in the form of the Soviet Union, and they were right on the firing line and that therefore they had interests which were very important, common interest with the United States.

Mr Rosenthal. I don't want to misappropriate your time, but do you think that that same leverage exists today or existed a week ago or 2 weeks ago? . . .

Mr Ball. Well, the whole question of American leverage with respect to Turkey, means taking a very serious view of a Turkish invasion to the point of denying aid, to the point of, in effect, telling the Turks what we told them in June 1964. This was a violation of a whole series of agreements and it called into question the whole idea of the NATO commitments as far as Turkey was concerned.

Mr Rosenthal. At that point the Greek junta had not yet fallen?

Mr Ball. That is right.

Mr Rosenthal. One could argue, just for the sake of discussion, that if the United States took that position, it would be implicitly supporting the junta in Athens?

Mr Ball. Let me say there was but one basis for the exercise of American leverage at that time. That was first to move against the junta. To say to the junta : 'You are finished as far as the United States is concerned unless you reverse this coup, unless you reinstall the legitimate government, the constitutional government, of Cyprus.' On that basis we would have had leverage with Turkey. That would have been very different from going to the Turks and saying, 'We are not going to do anything about this situation but we want you not to invade.' . . .

I agree with you entirely, Mr Chairman, that we had no leverage against the Turks unless we were prepared to denounce the junta's action in the first instance for bringing about this coup.

Mr Rosenthal. What I am leading up to is the more philosophical and general question : The administration has suggested before this committee that they were reluctant to issue public statements of denunciation because that would infringe on the private negotiations that were going on. I wonder what you think of that?

Mr Ball. In the first place, the private negotiations weren't successful, so I think we start with that.

As far as the Greek people were concerned, I personally think that they were waiting for a public signal of denunciation from the US Government. One of the problems in Greece has been a sense that the US Government was supporting the junta. There needed to be a public denunciation of this act, which was in violation of the accords, and inconsistent with Greece's NATO commitments.

It would have had to have been a public action to be in any way effective so the people would have been given something to respond to. Then we could have dealt with the Turks.

Mr Rosenthal. Could we have significantly helped resolve this situation by not taking sides either way?

Mr Ball. I don't think we would have been taking sides by saying to the Greeks : 'You have got to unscramble this coup and restore constitutional government.'

While saying to the Turks, 'You've got to hold off while we work this situation out.' That would not have been taking sides. I think we would have been performing the role we had performed successfully upon a number of occasions in the past. We never let the situation get out of hand as it seems to be out of hand at the moment.

Mr Rosenthal. Where do you see us today?

Mr Ball. Today the Turks occupy 40 per cent of the island—the best 40 per cent since because the northern coast is the great source of tourist revenue. It is the part of the island that is obviously the richest in that sense. Now, how we persuade the Turks to leave or even to reduce that 40 per cent to any extent commensurate with the proportion of the population that is Turkish, I think remains to be seen. I am not sure we can.

Actually the problem that we face right now is a very acute one. We have put almost insupportable pressures on the new Government in Athens . . .

175

We ought to give this democratic government in Greece a real chance. Instead, we are destroying it. We are destroying it as long as 40 per cent of Cyprus has been taken over by the Turks and all that we can say is that we would be glad to mediate.

For the United States to say that we are prepared to mediate shows an insensitivity which is beyond comprehension as far as I am concerned because the Government in Athens couldn't possibly accept mediation by the United States in view of the rapidly rising, dangerous anti-American feeling which has been generated in Greece by what has appeared to the Greek people as a pro-Turkish attitude on the part of America . . . The Greek Government in Athens is at the moment under pressures imposed by its humiliation at the hands of the Turks who simply walked in and took 40 per cent of Cyprus—and the Greeks had no possibility of a serious response. Cyprus is 600 miles away from Greece and 50 miles off the Turkish coast, out of the range of the Greek Air Force and the Turkish Air Force is very much larger. The only possible response would have been a fight in Thrace between Greece and Turkey which would have been disastrous for everybody.

Mr Rosenthal. Mr Wolff.

Mr Wolff. Thank you, Mr Chairman; (then addressing Mr Ball): I join with my colleagues who have before welcomed you to this committee, and the contributions you have made over a long period of time. I am troubled by the situation not only in Cyprus, but generally our relations between the United States and Greece and the United States and Turkey.

I have heard from time to time the expression used that Turkey is the eastern anchor of NATO and therefore we have got to make all sorts of concessions to the Turks in order to maintain their position as the eastern anchor.

It seems to me that anchor is dragging us down with it and dragging NATO with it because, if there is anything that has been a problem for NATO, it has been the recent situation that has developed with this war. If there is anything that is going to break NATO up, it is going to be this situation.

Do you think that we have to make great concessions to Turkey because of their particular position so far as NATO is concerned?

Mr Ball. I think we make a serious error even in the crassest terms of realpolitik to think Turkey has a special importance because it is the eastern anchor, and therefore we can permit a situation to develop between Turkey and its next door neighbor which is also a member of NATO, without doing irreparable harm to the whole fabric of NATO . . .

Pressures are likely to continue on the Greek Government where its only chance of survival may require it to ask for withdrawal of the American bases, for the withdrawal of all of our important intelligence installations there, asking that the fleet facilities be withdrawn from American use and so on. Well, this isn't building NATO or sustaining it; it seems to me it is beginning its demolition . . . It is a critical area when we have a Middle Eastern problem that could erupt into flames again. Suppose we have another Syrian attack on Israel. If at the same time we have deep troubles between the Greeks and the Turks, problems on the island, and nobody knows what effect this would have on Yugoslavia, we have a whole new set of problems.

Mr Findley. It is difficult to imagine a scenario more to the advantage of the Soviet Union in that part of the world.

Mr Ball. I agree.

Mr Findley. What levers do we have that can be effective in bringing about a better relationship in the NATO community on the southern flank?

Mr Ball. One of the problems is that because we have taken what appears to both the Greeks and the Turks as a hands-off attitude and which appears to the Greeks a pro-Turkish attitude, we have lost our leverage with Athens. Whatever leverage we have is only with Ankara. It is very difficult to play an effective role when you can affect only half the situation.

But I do think we are compelled nonetheless to make a serious try at it. Perhaps we ought to direct our fire primarily at Ankara in trying to get them to come forward with some sensible proposals . . .

Mr Rosenthal. Mr Yatron.

Mr Yatron. Thank you, Mr Chairman. Secretary Ball, it has been reported in the press and it is the view of many people, both in the United States as well as in Greece, that our country, our Government has tilted toward Turkey. If this is the case, if you feel this is the case, can you explain to me why our State Department would take this attitude, or this position?

Mr Ball. Well, when you say the State Department, I suppose you mean the Secretary of State, which is what the situation is at the moment?

Mr Yatron. Yes.

Mr Ball. I think it would be pure conjecture on my part to try to explain why Secretary Kissinger has taken the line he has. I would think that as much as anything it is a strategic calculation on his part that Turkey is more important than Greece. I don't want to do him an injustice by giving an oversimplified explanation. I think initially there may have been a feeling that the removal of Archbishop Makarios as the President of Cyprus was not a very bad thing . . .

Note by the author : In the body of this book, I have accused the former Greek royal house of having plotted with the Germans in World War One, acting against the expressed will of the Greek people. I added that there was evidence showing that the former Greek royal house acted not only out of natural Germanic feelings (they were related to the German royal house) but also because they received vast sums from Germany. The documents supporting these charges have been made public by the German Ministry of foreign affairs. Below I give the identifying numbers and dates of such documents, should anyone wish to consult them.

—Document No. 416, April 17, 1915, from Queen Sophia of Greece to her brother the Kaiser.

—File entitled 'Greek Royal Family', documents No. 359, 365, 1188.

—Document 18372, July 11, 1916. The German military attaché and General Metaxas, the military adviser and confidant of the King of Greece discuss the advisability of assassinating Eleftherios Venizelos, leader of the majority party in the Greek Parliament; and Metaxas recommends a joint German-Bulgarian attack on Greece.

—File A 28520, Documents 588 and 678, indicating that the King of Greece had received on his own account and for his own use —not for the use of his country—40 million marks.

—See also, in file marked Greek Royal Family, a letter to the Kaiser from King Constantine of Greece who offers to lead a joint German-Bulgarian force against Greece. At the time, Constantine had been deposed.

NOTES

1. When I left the brainwashing house, I made copious notes about all my experiences in Korea and all conversations. In my CAPTIVE IN KOREA, I explain how I smuggled these notes out on liberation.

2. US Ambassador Henry F. Grady, wrote a letter to the Greek Government in April 1950, asking for its resignation. Should the Government not resign, American aid would cease, the Ambassador wrote.

3. Upon my release from prison, I checked and found that the message I had received had indeed come from Mr Hearst.

4. Corroboration of this electoral fraud was given at the trial of the junta by, among others, General G. Koumanakos on August 7, 1975; by John Charalamboupoulos August 8, 1975; by John Alevras, August 6, 1975; Michael Papaconstantinou, August 6, 1975; Panayiotis Panourgias, Undersecretary of Transport in the Karamanlis government, August 2, etc.

5. I promised 'George' that his august mother would never hear of our outing. So, I will not give his name. His passion for cars is not a sufficient identifying characteristic. Such passion seems to reach epidemic proportions among members of royal families.

6. Manoli's circumstances are somewhat camouflaged: he does not want his family's misfortunes publicised by name: he feels that the rape of his sister is an unbearable shame to be hidden.

7. See any encyclopaedia, under 'Armenia', for what Turkey did to the people of that region in 1915. See also 'Keesing's Archives', 1955, for what the Turks did to the Greek minority in Istanbul in 1955.

8. Standard text of the oath of Athenian youths: my translation.

9. At the recent trial of the colonels in Athens, the presiding judge allowed testimony about American support of the junta but forbade the use of the names of the American officials concerned or the names of other persons who were not defendants but might be defendants at a later trial. I must abide by this ruling.

10. I was not the only one to whom the Americans praised Papadopoulos. In testimony during the trial of the junta, on August 12, 1975, Colonel Nicolas Hondrokoukis and Colonel Antonios Papaspyrou among many others reported similar remarks. The judge did not allow them to give the names of the Americans in question.

11. Andreas Papandreou is the source of this information. He has made the statement publicly and it has been printed in *LE NOUVEL OBSERVATEUR*.

12. That Mr Garoufalias protected the coup leaders was confirmed during the trial of the junta on August 6, 1975 in testimony by Mr Michael Papaconstantinou who served as Undersecretary of Defence under Mr Garoufalias.

13. For the facts on Aspida see the testimony of Colonel Alexander Papaterpos at the trial of the junta, August 7, 1975.

14. See note 13, above.

15. Testimony by George Lianis at the junta trial, August 9, 1975.

16. For the testimony linking American officials with these activities see the record of the junta trial : testimony by Alexander Lykourezos.

17. Testimony by General Michael Opropoulos at the junta trial, August 4, 1975.

18. Testimony by Mr Michael Papaconstantinou at the junta trial, August 6, 1975.

19. The man in question is under indictment. I cannot reveal his name.

20. I made a record of the conversation immediately and I think I have it verbatim.

21. I can only surmise that Adlai Stevenson had been unnerved by the prospect of working for Lyndon Johnson, a man he despised.

22. I made a record of George Papandreou's words.

23. The terms of Mr Acheson's proposal can be found in Keesing's Archives for 1965.

24. I have given extracts here of Ambassador Matsas' report.

25. Testimony at the junta trial on August 6 by Mr Michael Papaconstantinou, former Undersecretary of Defence.

26. Ibid.

27. Corroborating documents were introduced in evidence at the junta trial.

28. See *Washington Post*, May 15, 1967 for a description of this meeting. Neither Professor Rostow nor the White House denied the *Washington Post* story. See also the testimony at the Junta trial on August 8, 1975 by Mr George Mylonas, member of the Greek Parliament.

29. Admiral K. Engolfopoulos, C. in C. of the Greek Navy at the time of the coup testified at the junta's trial on July 30th and

completely corroborated the story of Mr Canellopoulos. No witness cast doubt on that testimony.

30. Through the month of August 1975, a parade of witnesses testified at the trial of the torturers—Minis was one of the witnesses. His treatment is typical. I chose him because his story came out first. Several of the torturers have confessed and thrown themselves on the mercy of the court.

31. Moustaklis appeared at the trial of his torturers on August 18, 1975. He could hardly speak or move but he showed the marks on his body.

PHILIP DEANE (Philippe Deane Gigantes), born 1923, served in the Royal Navy as a Navigator during World War II. After the war he became a journalist representing *The Observer* in Greece, North Africa and South Asia. While reporting for his paper in Korea he was captured by the Communists, remaining a prisoner for 33 months. Upon release he wrote *Captive in Korea,* thereafter resuming his journalistic career and eventually becoming Washington correspondent for *The Observer* and *The Toronto Globe and Mail.* He left journalism to work successively as a U.N. official, Secretary General to King Constantine of Greece, Greek Minister of Culture, and television commentator. Then, at 44, he went to university in Canada for the first time, emerging with a Ph.D. in Classics. He subsequently served as Dean of two universities, and is at present studying for a degree in Economics.